MW01280020

LETTERS FROM HAVANA

LCMS Vicar Writes Home During the Cuban Revolution 1957-58

David V. Dissen

Edited by
Cheryl D. Naumann

Letters from Havana
LCMS Vicar Writes Home During the Cuban Revolution 1957-58
By David V. Dissen
Edited by Cheryl D. Naumann

2021 © David V. Dissen

ISBN: 978-1-935035-33-6

All Bible quotations are from the New King James Version, Thomas Nelson, Nashville, TN, 1982, 1984.

Kindle Direct Publishing

Dedicated

First and foremost, to the glory of the true and
Triune God: Father, Son and Holy Spirit; three
distinct persons in one Divine Being and essence;

To my parents, who raised their children in the
saving faith of Jesus Christ and kept us rooted and
grounded in the holy, inspired, inerrant and
infallible truths of God's Word;

And to my beloved wife, Judy,
who shares that same Christian faith.

Jesus said to His disciples: "Go therefore and make disciples of all the nations, baptizing them in the name of the Father and of the Son and of the Holy Spirit, teaching them to observe all things that I have commanded you; and lo, I am with you always, even to the end of the age" (Matt. 28:19-20).

God promised His people in Isaiah 55:11 that when His Word is proclaimed, it will not return to Him empty, but it will accomplish what He wants and achieve what He has in mind. With that unbreakable promise, we Christians unashamedly proclaim His holy, inspired, inerrant, infallible, and efficacious Word wherever we are and in whatever station in life God has placed us. Our prayer as Christians is that those who hear God's Word and do not yet believe will have their eyes opened, "in order to turn them from darkness to light, and from the power of Satan to God, that they may receive forgiveness of sins and an inheritance among those who are sanctified by faith" in Christ Jesus (Acts 26:18).

CONTENTS

ACKNOWLEDGEMENTS

First, I want to express my thanks to my sainted father, Rev. Victor Herman von Dissen (he dropped "von" from his name during World War II) and for my sainted mother, Lydia. They had the fore-sight to save my "Letters from Havana" during my vicarage in Cuba, when Fidel Castro was leading what later proved to be a successful revolt against Dictator Fulgencio Batista.

I also want to express my thanks to my dear and supportive wife Judy Dissen (née Bentrott, from Lowden, Iowa) of more than 50 years; to Michelle Christ (formerly Executive-Assistant to the President of Concordia Seminary, St. Louis, when I served on the Board of Regents, and who is now the Executive-Assistant to the President of the LCMS Missouri District); to Beth Glaus (Director of the Department of Public Safety at Southeast Missouri State University in Cape Girardeau); to Deaconess Cheryl D. Naumann who, along with her husband Rev. Dr. Jonathan C. Naumann, serves as a missionary in the Dominican Republic and Latin America; and to our own pastor, Rev. Wayne Scwhiesow, who serves Zion Lutheran Church in Gordonville, Missouri. They all encouraged me to keep and publish these letters.

The "LETTERS FROM HAVANA" WERE NOT ORIGINALLY INTENDED FOR THE PUBLIC. Therefore, I have made some edits and also some additions/deletions for purely "personal reasons." Hopefully those who read these "LETTERS FROM HAVANA" will gain some insights about the life of a vicar and the mission work of our LCMS in Cuba during Fidel Castro's Revolution. If anyone should be offended by anything that I have written, then I ask God's forgiveness for Jesus' sake, and the forgiveness of anyone who is offended. I thank God daily for His forgiving grace in Christ Jesus, Whose shed blood on Calvary cleanses all believers in Him from all sins and gives all believers in Him the unbreakable promise of the resurrection to eternal life in heaven.

Rev. David V. Dissen,

SOLI DEO GLORIA!!!

FOREWORD

As a young boy born in 1956, I grew up in the middle of the Cold War. I remember how the specter of nuclear war was a constant companion of my childhood, with testing of the Emergency Broadcast System and the construction of bomb shelters all over town. A part of the danger that we faced was the threat of Fidel Castro's Cuba sitting on our doorstep, not more than 90 miles off the coast of Florida. Who can forget the Bay of Pigs fiasco or the Cuban Missile Crisis? And then there was the constant stream of Cuban refugees who risked everything to flee from the tyranny of Castro's Cuba to the freedom of the United States of America!

Still, Cuba remained an unknown quantity to me until I met the Rev. David Dissen in Cape Girardeau, Missouri. It wasn't long before I learned that he had the dubious honor of serving out his vicarage in Cuba during Castro's revolution. He spoke of the dangers that he faced on several occasions and, through his reminiscences, I began to gain an appreciation for what it was like for the people living there during that distressing time.

It was with great interest that I heard about the letters that he had written home during his vicarage year in Havana and, along with others, I encouraged him to make the letters available to the world for posterity's sake. I'm glad that I did and I'm glad that he did! They are a valuable source of insight into what was taking place at that critical time in world history! History books give only the facts about Castro's revolution, but Pastor Dissen's letters make that history come alive! Dealing with ordinary things, they provide a unique window into what everyday life was like, even as the world around him was unraveling. They reveal the truth that even in the midst of great trouble there is joy to be found; even in the midst of a violent revolution there is life to be lived and there are souls to be saved!

It is my hope and my fervent prayer that readers will find as much interest and delight in these LETTERS FROM HAVANA as I did myself!

Pastor Wayne W. Schwiesow
Zion and St. Paul Lutheran Churches
Gordonville and Chaffee, Missouri

FOREWORD 2

I was born in 1958 and have lived in the same community, the same house even, for my entire life. Life in Cape Girardeau, Missouri, was quiet and uneventful and I knew nothing at all about Cuba. With only two houses on our country road, the lives of my family and the family next door were simple and easy. It was in October 1962 when I first became aware of Cuba and recall watching the construction of a concrete room in our neighbor's basement. Following its construction, practice drills took us hurriedly next door, timing each exercise to shave minutes off our official time. Time passed and we never had to scamper next door for real. As the 1960s moved on, the memories of that concrete room also moved on and I gave it little thought.

Those memories surfaced years later during a campus Bible study at the Lutheran Chapel of Hope at Southeast Missouri State University. The pastor, Rev. David Dissen, had retired from Trinity Lutheran Church in Cape Girardeau and was serving as Chaplain. During the Bible study he shared an experience from his vicarage in Cuba. I asked when he was there and recalled it being months before I was born. I tried to refresh my memory of history to pin down exactly what was happening in Cuba during that time, but quickly put it aside, thinking to myself – and telling Pastor Dissen – you should write a book about your time there. He thought it may not be relevant to anyone and continued the Bible study. Other students found his story interesting as well, but we didn't discuss it further, chuckling to learn that Pastor, a young seminarian planning for a vicarage in the States (likely someplace north) wound up in Cuba with only a suitcase, a portable typewriter and the clothes he was wearing.

Years passed and I reminded Pastor Dissen a few times that he should write about his experiences in Cuba. One day, on a dreary late December afternoon, I got a phone call from him, sharing that he wrote to his parents nearly every week during his vicarage, and that his mother had saved every letter. He went on to tell me he found the letters while he was cleaning up some files. I thought, what luck – seems like there is no excuse not to write about his time in Cuba! By the time our conversation was over, I believed for the first time that this project was really going to happen.

But luck had nothing to do with it. Every detail of one's life is ordered by God and these events in the life of Pastor Dissen serve as examples of that very fact. In Jeremiah 29:11 we are reminded, "For I know the plans I have for you," declares the LORD, "plans to prosper you and not to harm you, plans to give you hope and a future." Pastor Dissen was placed in Cuba at a specific time and wrote about his experiences in letters that his mother saved, to fulfill God's plan not only for Pastor Dissen, but also for the readers of this collection.

Pastor Dissen's work in Cuba prepared him for his future as a pastor in The Lutheran Church - Missouri Synod and was used by the Holy Spirit to share the Good News of Christ's love for us. This preparation happened during a time of historic global significance, but as *Letters from Havana* reveal, sharing the Gospel is a daily routine. It should be recognized as habit in one's life, regardless of one's vocation or location. It is shared during peaceful quiet times with friends and to the masses during the rise and fall of regimes. Isaiah 55:8-11 describes it best: "For My thoughts are not your thoughts, neither are your ways My ways," declares the LORD. "As the heavens are higher than the earth, so are My ways higher than your ways and My thoughts than your thoughts. As the rain and the snow come down from heaven, and do not return to it without watering the earth and making it bud and flourish, so that it yields seed for the sower and bread for the eater, so is My word that goes out from My mouth: It will not return to Me empty but will accomplish what I desire and achieve the purpose for which I sent it."

This was true in the life of a young Lutheran vicar who found himself in Cuba in 1957 and remains true in his life in 2021. In the simple observations of this layperson, it remains true for us all because God knows the plans He has for us - to share the Gospel of Christ through His Word, which He will nourish in the hearts of those who hear it; because His Word will not return empty – whether it is in a time of historic significance or in a loving, simple letter, written home.

Beth Ramey Glaus
Director of Department of Public Safety
Southeast Missouri State University, Cape Girardeau

FOREWORD 3

I met Pastor Dissen more than 15 years ago, when he served on the Board of Regents for Concordia Seminary in St. Louis, and I served as an executive assistant to the president. We connected immediately over our mutual respect and care for first responders, which launched many conversations about life, service to our fellow man, and the love of Jesus for all.

At one of our early Board dinners, some of the pastors were discussing their time as students at the seminaries of the LCMS. This led to stories about their Vicarage years when seminarians begin to put their first two years of seminary education to work in a church or mission setting. Pastor Dissen's stories captivated me. He casually mentioned that he served his Vicarage in Havana, Cuba, in 1957-58, during the Castro revolution. I was stunned. No wonder I couldn't get enough of his stories!

Whenever we had down time at Board meetings, I'd say, "Tell me about your vicarage." His recollections were always so rich with the history of that time. He would paint the picture in my mind of the beauty of Cuba and her people while telling of the people living through both the hope and horror of such a revolution.

It wasn't long before I was encouraging him to write down his experiences. I've always felt he needed to share them, and I hated that they might someday be lost. Pastor Dissen's memories and stories are not just of the history of Cuba and her people during the Castro revolution. His words are of the true hope that comes from Jesus Christ, for the people of Cuba in 1957-58, and for you and me today and always.

I am so excited that he has decided to share these letters written during his Vicarage. More than sixty years later, he is still sharing his stories of Cuba and the love of Jesus. As each of us opens this book, we can all say, "Tell me about your vicarage."

Michelle Christ
Executive-Assistant to the President
LCMS Missouri District

PROLOGUE

During my third year at Concordia Seminary, I had my pre-vicarage interview and was asked if I would have any objections to serving in a foreign vicarage for 1957-1958. The Seminary was considering sending several vicars to a foreign vicarage and I was being considered for one of them. I said something to the effect, "I've been trained to serve in the Lord's Kingdom. The Lord is the Commander-In-Chief and Head of the Holy Christian Church. I am ready to serve wherever He sends me."

My initial vicarage assignment was to Good Shepherd Lutheran Congregation in Mexico City, Mexico. Prior to leaving for Mexico, the Missouri Synod's Mission Department enrolled me in a 10-day intensive course in Spanish at the Berlitz School of Language in St. Louis.

I went home to spend a few days with my parents in Union Grove, Wisconsin. I had already sent a trunk and suit-case load of materials to the Mexican border. I was supposed to pick up the trunk and suit-case at the border and continue on to Mexico City. My railroad ticket had been purchased. My suit-case for Mexico was packed. I had a portable typewriter as a carry-on.

About 48 hours before I was scheduled to leave for Mexico, I received a phone call from the Seminary and the Synod's Mission Department. They informed me that there was a change of plans, and that I would be going to Havana, Cuba, instead of Mexico City. They said not to worry about getting my trunk and suitcase. They would re-route them to Havana. However, the current missionary in Cuba, Rev. Eugene Gruell, was now on vacation in the U.S. with his family and would NOT be there to meet me and pick me up at the airport, but a church member would be there. Thus, I would be on "my own" for a couple of weeks.

I arrived at the Miami International Airport about 1 a.m. on the morning of Sunday August 4, 1957. Since I had no place to catch some sleep except at the airport, and since I wasn't too tired yet, I found an open shop at the airport where I bought and then sent the following post-card to my parents. It read: "Dear all: Arrived in Miami 1 a.m. Sunday morning on the

Silver Falcon. Due in at Havana at 9 a.m. this Sunday morning. Hope I can keep awake in church as I've had no sleep. No hotel room and is too hard to sleep at Airport. Probably sleep all day Monday. Tremendous flight so far. Everything fine. Dave."

When I deplaned at Havana International Airport and entered the terminal, I was wondering how I would make contact with the church member, when a gentleman approached me and asked if I was Vicar Dissen. I said: "Yes." He said: "My name is Mr. Peterson and I am here to pick you up and get you settled in." He said he easily identified me in the crowd of arriving passengers because he had been told to look for a young, blonde American man with a crew-cut. I believe I was the only blonde with a crew cut who had de-planed.

I stayed at the Peterson's house in Havana for about 10 days and then stayed at the home of Mr. and Mrs. Herr in Havana until the Gruell family returned. For the first month or so I lived out of my suit-case, until my trunk and other suit-case arrived and I had access to more clothes and some of my books.

These were some of the twists and turns before and after I arrived at my vicarage destination. I thoroughly enjoyed my foreign vicarage. I hope you will enjoy learning more about my vicarage in Havana during the Castro revolution in "LETTERS FROM HAVANA."

1

AUGUST 1957

Dear Dad and Ma,

Just a few lines to fill you in on some of my activities since leaving home. As you know from the post card (that is, if Uncle Sam delivered it), I left St. Louis last Saturday evening for Havana. I got into Miami about 1 a.m. Sunday morning. Since no sleeping quarters were provided, I walked around and kept busy until my departure for Havana at 8 a.m. The plane ride to Miami was really wonderful. It's really a thrill to see God's handiwork above the clouds and to look from the towering heights down on His creation. It is a thrill and a joy that calls for a definite repeat performance on my return home to the States.

I did have a little trouble in Miami. When I confirmed my flight reservation to Havana, the ticket agent made me purchase a round trip ticket to Miami. Otherwise, he said that customs inspection in Havana would not permit me to enter the country. Reason: Everyone coming to Cuba must have a ticket out of the country or sufficient money (several hundred dollars) to guarantee their ability to leave the country in case an emergency demands it. I bought the round-trip ticket.

I arrived in Havana about 9:20 a.m. and was met at the airport by one of the members, a Mr. Peterson. First, I had to clear customs with my suit-case and typewriter. That was no trouble at all. I happened to notice one customs inspector who wasn't even checking the suitcases. All he had the people do was open their packages and then he would slap an okay on them. I went over there and it was only a matter of seconds before I was cleared.

I had a chance to wash up a bit before going to church. Church was at 11:00, with the vicar from the Isle of Pines preaching. There is no church building in Havana. They rent one side of an apartment house for our place of worship. It seats about 40 but there were only about 20 in attendance at the English service.

Sunday afternoon Mr. Peterson and his family took the vicar and me for a ride through Havana. Conditions (traffic) certainly are different than those in the U.S. They have no arterial stops here (I suppose Fred and Mart would like that) and very few traffic signals. At intersections it is dog eat dog. That explains the many cracked up cars and dented fenders one sees in Havana. Also, when a person toots his horn it means: "Stay where you are buddy, I am going to pass you on one side or the other." They observe no proper lane turning. As long as someone is in front of you, you can expect them to do anything. They may make a left-hand turn from a right-hand lane and vice versa. Or they may decide to stop smack dab in the middle of the street and talk with a friend whom they happen to see. Pedestrians and bicyclists are also very careless. You can be traveling along at 30 or 40 m.p.h. and suddenly you will see a pedestrian walk right in front of you or a bicyclist dart out of an intersection. Honking the horn doesn't help one bit because they just don't move. At any rate, it amazes me to see the utter disregard these pedestrians have for their safety. Maybe they want to get hit and then have the driver support them for the remainder of their life.

Mr. Peterson took us through downtown Havana. That includes Old Havana and New Havana. Old Havana reminds one of the middle ages. The roads, stores and buildings are very archaic. We also drove past President Batista's palace. I must say that it did seem strange to see about 20 guards out in front walking back and forth, all armed with tommy-guns. As a matter of fact, many of the regular policeman carry tommy-guns. It isn't too difficult to have it impressed upon you that you are living in a country under a dictator.

After driving around for a couple of hours, we stopped for refreshments at some corner stand. We were able to get Cokes. As I left, some ragged Cuban youngster followed after me and kept saying, "Money, money!" I guess that was the only English word he knew. Mr. Peterson told me this was a common occurrence, that in the thinking of Cubans, all Americans are made of money. He got rid of the little boy for me by telling him: "Quite se," which means, "Get Lost!"

In the evening we sat out on the Peterson's sun porch which overlooks the bay. They live only a quarter of a block from the bay and is it ever beautiful in the evening. It almost seems like a summer paradise. You can look out and see the boats coming in and going out. All you can see is water for miles. Really a wonderful view. I know Dad would love it. They do quite a bit of fishing from the shore.

The Peterson's are a very nice family. They come from Fort Worth, Texas. He works at the Government Embassy and has been here about a year. They have two young children, a boy about eight and a girl about eleven. They have a Cuban maid and live in a nice apartment, as you have probably already gathered. They try to live as American as possible, which naturally costs much more. American foods are much higher here than in the States. For example, cheese here costs $0.65 a half pound for Velveeta or $2.15 for a 2-pound box. You can see I won't be eating much cheese. I'll probably be staying with the Peterson's until Sunday and then move over with the Herr's. Paster Gruell (who is on vacation right now) wants me to stay with the Peterson's and Herr's until he gets back from his vacation. He knows his Spanish well and figures he can be very helpful to me in finding a reasonable apartment. I guess he'll be back about the 21st or 22nd.

Also, I have already eaten several Cuban dishes. So far, they have really been tasty. I ate fresh pineapple for the first time, and it is D E L I C I O U S. It tastes nothing like canned pineapple. Fried green bananas are also good. I don't care too much for the way Cubans fix their rice but guess I can eat it.

I met with Pastor Gruell in St. Louis last week Thursday and we more or less laid out my field of work. He said he wants to work strictly with the Spanish. Therefore, he is turning over to me the entire English-German element of the congregation. I am to be responsible for all the English sermons, teach the Bible Class, supervise the Sunday School and preach at Hershey every Friday night. Hershey is a mission about 50 miles out of Havana. This work will keep me plenty busy. All I am doing now is preaching Sundays, keeping the Sunday School together and teaching Bible Class. He said he doesn't want me to make calls until he gets back; that he is satisfied if I just take care of the preaching. My sermon for this Sunday has kept me plenty busy so far. I first finished the final draft tonight. That gives me three days in which to study it.

Things have sort of been popping around here since Batista

3

withdrew all Constitutional rights last Thursday. We never read about it in the local newspapers unless it is something so big that many of the residents of Havana know about it. Otherwise, the newspapers are censored. It is almost an every-day occurrence to buy a U.S. newspaper that has one or more articles clipped out of it because it says something it shouldn't say. Mr. Petersen has a short wave set in the room in which I'm staying. Every morning and evening we can pick up Key West, Florida. Sometimes we hear things that have leaked out of Cuba that aren't announced over the stations in Cuba.

Especially this week, things have been literally popping. Yesterday three bombs were set off in Havana. One was in the largest dime store, F.W. Woolworths. Three people were critically injured and five others less seriously. Everyone knew about this bombing, so the papers and commentators carried it. The other two were not so widely circulated but Mr. Petersen heard about them at the U.S. Embassy. Then, this afternoon about 4:00, I was sitting in the front room checking my sermon when I heard a loud explosion. Camilla (Petersen's girl) said she thought it was thunder (it looked like rain at the time) but I told her it was too loud for thunder. Sure enough, about ten minutes later Mrs. Petersen came in all breathless and shaking like a leaf. She had just been on her way back home from downtown Havana where she takes Spanish lessons every day from 3:00 – 4:00. There is a tunnel under the river connecting our section of town (Miramar) with downtown Havana. Mrs. Petersen had just passed through the tunnel when a bomb went off in the tunnel on the opposite side. It closed down all traffic in the tunnel heading out of the downtown section. Traffic heading into downtown Havana was not blocked because there are two separate tunnels, one for outbound traffic and one for inbound traffic. We were through this tunnel several times on our sight-seeing trip Sunday.

There is no need to worry about me or get any gray hairs, though. The only time you can expect trouble is when a bomb goes off or if there is shooting and you are foolish enough to investigate or get curious. The best thing to do when things are popping is to keep in your room. That is what we at the Petersen house have been doing. We only go out for necessities. As a result, I haven't gotten to know Cuba too well but maybe when things die down a little, I'll have a chance.

I have had no news on my trunk as yet. It has been a week now since I turned the problem of getting it over to Havana to the Railway Express Agency. It's hard telling when I'll get it. Until then, I just live on the clothes I had in my suit-case.

By the way, you can address letters to me in care of Pastor Gruell. The address, if you lost it is:

Rev. E. H. Gruell
Calle B. No. 106, Apto. 3
entre Ir a y 3r a, La Puntilla
Miramar, La Habana, Cuba

In case I failed to mention it, Pastor Gruell is from Wisconsin. He was born in Janesville, Wisconsin and planned to go there from St. Louis. He even preached in Union Grove, in 1943. He knows Uncle Wally and cousin Elaine. Guess Elaine doubled with him a few times before she married Jack. Elaine knows both Pastor and his wife well.

Can't complain on the weather so far. It is very humid but not as hot as St. Louis. Could be that spending a month and a half in St. Louis prepared me for this weather.

I saw baseball on TV last night. Havana and Rochester were playing in Havana. They have some pretty good players on both teams. It was a wonderfully pitched game. Rochester won it in 11 innings, 2 to 1.

Dave

P.S. Perhaps you can pass this letter on to Walt and Bill later on. I don't know when I'll get a chance to write them. Besides, air mail from Havana to the States is $.14 a letter. That is providing you buy your stamps at the post office in downtown Havana. Otherwise, you pay about $.17 per stamp. You know how it is, the stores have to have a handling charge.

Dear Dad and Ma,

I was glad to get your letter of the 4th yesterday but sorry to hear about Dad's rupture and Ma's being down again. You're both old enough to know your limitations. However, I thought Dad had pledged not to work at the County Fair this year.

This morning I moved over with the Herr's until Pastor Gruell gets back. He should be back sometime next week. Then with his help he wants me to find my own room or apartment. It sure will be good to settle down and be able to unpack and stay for a-while. Living out of the suit-case gets frustrating after a-while.

By the way, I hope you checked on the airmail postage to Havana. I say this because I noticed that you sent your letter in an air mail envelope. However, it did not arrive at Gruell's until yesterday. In other words, it took about nine days via air mail. It seems like rather slow service to me but if air mail is that bad, I wonder what the regular first-class mail is like.

On Sunday, I attended my first Spanish service. There were only four who were present but it was a thrill to worship with them. They sang as well as the thirty did who were present at the English service. Naturally, I did not understand much of the sermon, but the liturgy and the singing of the hymns I was able to follow and understand. After all, a ten-day intensive course in Spanish does not make you fluent in that language. I doubt it very much if I'll ever preach in Spanish here. The Cubans talk too rapidly and swallow too many words. I suppose it would be boring for them to have to listen to a North American try and preach in their language.

Bible Class and Sunday School were rather poorly attended but then that was understandable. Pastor Gruell had postponed Sunday School and Bible Class for the month of August because he thought no one would be here to take care of them. Their first notification of the change of plans was last Sunday, and there were very few present in either service. Several English-speaking Cubans were present in the Bible Class. One in particular, a very personable young man, seemed to be interested in our church, even though he is not a member. If he does join, it looks like the church will have a good worker.

Sunday afternoon the Peterson's took me out to dinner, along with the Herr's. We had a real Cuban dinner – chicken and rice or "arroz con pollo" in Spanish. We ate at one of the Cuban night clubs, the Rancho Luna (Ranch of the Moon). It is typically Cuban. It's open on all four sides with a sloping roof of Cuban thatched grass. Palm trees on all four sides serve as the only walls. On the one end is the bar and thereafter are the tables. It must easily seat 150-200 people. As for the food, it was simply delicious. The only thing was, there was so much of it and so many different kinds that one could not eat it all. By the time you finished your chicken and rice you had a hard time eating the French-fries, fried green bananas (which take the place of potatoes in Cuba and are very good) and fried ripe bananas. Then there is your salad with tomatoes, cucumbers, avocados and lettuce. And don't forget the Cuban beer. It was my first Cuban beer and very good. After the desert (strawberry ice cream), we had Cuban coffee and crème de coconut. It was my first try at drinking Cuban coffee and WOW, is it ever potent! They serve it to you in a very small cup (about two good swallows) and it is as strong as you'll ever drink. It is also very bitter and requires the adding of several teaspoons of sugar. When you have it ready, you close your eyes and gulp it down. Then drink some water. Believe me, it makes your hair stand on end.

There have been very few bombings since Sunday so maybe things are cooling off. I have yet to go downtown for a real good look but I hope that will be next week. A week from Sunday I don't have to preach. On Monday morning, I was over at the Church office. One certainly can't do much work while he is there. The bell is ringing all the time. Either people want to sell you something or else they are begging. I walked around the neighborhood by the church to became acquainted. I found a shoeshine stand where for "diez centavos" (ten cents) you can get a shine that will beat any two-bit shine in the States. I had mine shined since my polish and stuff is in my trunk.

By the way, if you have a good map of Cuba, you should easily be able to see where I was staying when I lived with the Peterson's. Pastor and his family live in the same apartment. It is on the point of the Rio Almendares

(Almendares River). That is why the address is La Puntilla, meaning the point. The apartment is right on the corner of this point so you can see what a wonderful view of the ocean that you have from it. I only wish I wouldn't have had to work so long on my sermon. Then I could have enjoyed the stay there much more.

I hope to find some halfway decent wedding anniversary card for you but so far I have had no success. They tell me that Havana is like Old Mother Hubbard's Cupboard when it comes to occasional cards.

I see where the Braves have really put some daylight between themselves and the closest team. Those Cardinals were very obliging in this last series. And with Adcock ready in about two weeks the Braves just may be set. Of course, there is still plenty of time.

By the way, don't ever send anything to me. Customs is much too high and it would never be worth the cost.

Dave

Vicar David V. Dissen

Dear Dad and Ma,

Well, another new week in Cuba and more experiences about which to write. I just finished working on my today's diary, even though it is yet only afternoon. As long as I'm at my typewriter, I may as well continue.

This week is a little easier on me. Pastor Gruell is supposed to return this week and according to the schedule he gave me in the States, I do not have to preach this Sunday. Therefore, this has been one week so far (only two days into the week) that I have done a few things that would not have been possible to do if I had a sermon to prepare for Sunday.

Sunday morning there was a rather good attendance at the English service – close to 30. I pulled one rather humorous blunder about which I will long be able to chuckle. I am accustomed to Elsie or Mrs. Richter playing the "Create in me etc." They immediately begin playing after the Votum but the organist here did not. She is an elderly lady and is very slow and hesitant about playing. After saying the Votum, I turned to the altar to wait for her to start playing. When she didn't play and didn't play, I took the offering plate and turned around, thinking that she had forgotten. Just as I turned around with the offering plate in hand, she began to play. The usher returned to his seat. There I stood, facing the congregation with collection plate in hand, while the congregation sang "Create in me." It was while I was standing there that some of the members literally brought their offerings to the altar during the singing and dropped their offerings in the plate as I stood facing them. I guess they thought it was a new way of taking the offering or something. I noticed that several of the American people had all they could do to restrain from laughing out loud. It was rather humorous.

Sunday afternoon the Herr's (at whose house I'll now be staying until I find my apartment) took me out towards Hershey to give me an idea of the road that I'll often be traveling. The first 20 miles is on well paved, four lane highway, called the Via Blanca. It's a very beautiful drive. The Via Blanca runs along the Ocean and the many palm trees and tropical vegetation add to the scenic drive. However, after about 20 miles you suddenly hit a very narrow dirt road. There is room for two-way traffic to pass and that is all. The road is full of chuck holes. After a short distance on this road, you descend a rather steep, narrow hill and you are suddenly at the edge of the ocean in a very poor village called Boca de Jaruco. It was in this village that slightly over a year ago Ernest Hemingway filmed his movie picture "The Old Man and the Sea." It is a very small village and typically Latin American. There are two streets through the place and that's it. Both are very narrow. There are shanty homes right alongside. They are wooden frame houses but are no more than shells. You can look in one side and see out through the other without the doors being opened (those that have doors). Inside these homes, you can see the filth and dirt in which these people live. You can see their bedrooms and bunks on the floor. You can see their kitchen and that's about it. On the front porch, you will see pigs, chickens, cows, goats and other animals. I can see why Hemingway picked this place because it is a regular Ocean type village. In case I failed to mention it in my previous correspondence, Hemingway's son lives in the hotel directly across from the Peterson's apartment. Ernest stays with him whenever he is in Havana, which is usually from November until April or May. I have seen both his son and his son's wife at a distance.

Getting back to this village of Boca de Jaruco. You only go about two blocks thru the village (that's it period) when you make a sharp turn to the left and make a practically 90° descent down another hill which is wide enough for only one-way-traffic. After making the descent, you are now at Ocean level. There is a small inlet down here which necessitates crossing a one-way wooden bridge. And what a bridge. It is some lumber across the water, with no guard rails or side protection whatsoever, just wide enough for a car to cross. It is a little scary when you cross this bridge. After crossing it, you have several miles more of dirt road and then you once again hit pavement. I guess that it is supposed to be pavement from here on in, all the way to Hershey. We didn't go into Hershey but it was far enough to let me know about how to get there. I should really have some experiences going to this mission station. I hope to get plenty of pictures all the way along, especially in Boca de Jaruco. It should prove to be very interesting.

Yesterday morning I took my first bus ride into downtown Havana. I stopped off at one of the F.W. Woolworth stores and went in to price things. Wow! Practically everything was at least double or more than it was in the States. I also stopped at the record department to look at and price their records. I found out that their records were $6.75 a piece for LP's (which are $3.95 in the States). I also found out that the record clerk was a very pretty and friendly Cuban gal. She spoke to me in Spanish at first but I had a hard time understanding her because she spoke so fast. Finally, she said a few words in English so then we were okay. I found out she was trying to learn English and since I was trying to learn Spanish, we helped each other out. In the meantime, she was playing all the American records they had.

From this F.W. Woolworth store, I boarded a bus and went down into Old Havana. This was about 12:30 and I had completely forgotten about the stores being closed from 12:30 until 2:30 for their siestas. As a result, when I got downtown the stores were all closed. I got off at their biggest Woolworth store, the one that was bombed two weeks ago. All I could do was walk around and look, though, since everything was closed. Finally, I boarded a bus about 1:30 and came back home.

This morning I went down to the U.S. Embassy. I registered so that in case anything ever happened to me they knew that I was living in Cuba for about a year. I also found out that if I remain in Havana as a tourist, at the end of six months I'll have to return to the States for a couple of hours. That would be on Feb. 2 or thereabouts.

From the Embassy, Mrs. Herr took me to the custom's brokers office to check on my trunk and suit-case. I had information from the Missouri Pacific R.R. last Saturday that they had shipped it and it was on its way. This morning I found out at the custom's broker that my trunk and suit-case were indeed in Havana already. He told me to call him Friday and then he'll find out where I want it delivered. I hope to be able to wait until I find my own apartment or room but that all depends upon when Pastor Gruell returns.

From the Custom's Brokers office, Mrs. Herr took me to see the Columbus Cathedral, the largest Catholic Cathedral in Cuba and their only Cathedral in Havana. It is made of limestone, marble and some other type of sandstone. It's over 200 years old and still in very good shape. A priest served as our guide through the Cathedral and their museum. He pointed out their mahogany cabinets that were as old as the church and still very good. I also saw a statue of Christopher Columbus who is the patron saint of Havana. On the left wall in the chancel, they have a memorial plaque which supposedly is the place where Columbus' bones are now resting. Hanging on the ceiling between the chancel and nave is a very huge, crystal glass chandelier. He turned these lights on and it is simply magnificent. The chandelier is about twenty feet in height and weighs over a ton. This gives you some idea of how large it is, and it is crystal glass only.

In their museum we saw many interesting articles. They had many of the old Cuban coins, curios, etc. Also, I found out that Santa Barbara was the patron saint of limestone. That, according to the priest, is where Santa Barbara, California, derived its name.

After our tour of the Cathedral, we went across the street in front of the cathedral, across a parking lot and into the Havana Club. But this parking lot, in itself, is very historical. It is square. It is surrounded on all sides by buildings that served as the slave market in "Old Havana." In the center of the parking-lot, you can see circular marks which outline the circular, elevated platform of the old slave market. On the sides of this circle, you can see triangles coming out on all sides. These triangles are bordered by a rather narrow, circular walk (still plainly visible), which surround the circular platform in the center. The platform is where the slave buyer's "spotters" stood; the triangles are where the slaves were kept; and the circular walk is where those who were buying the slaves stood. The slave buyers had their spotters standing on the circular platform and they would point out to their bosses the best slaves. Then, when bidding on the slaves started, the slave buyers would bid only on those slaves that their spotters had pointed out to them.

In front of the Havana Club are many curio shops and souvenir peddlers. I bought my first Cuban souvenirs here. One fellow was selling Rhumba Doll Bracelets made from coconut seeds. He wanted $1.00 for 3 of them but I told him no, I wanted 4. Finally, he agreed so I was able to buy 4 for $1.00. Later I learned that the same type of bracelet sold in the stores from anywhere between $.50 and $1.00 each. Guess it was a pretty good buy. Another fellow was selling castanets at 3 for $1.00. I figured that these would make a good gift for Ronnie and Carol but I only wanted two of them. Finally, he agreed to sell me two, with their names carved on them, for $.60. I took him up on it. They certainly were worth $.30 each. Also did pricing of other curios in the curio shops, but in the shops things are much higher. For instance, I priced a brief case at $29.75 and another one at $43.00 and some odd cents. That was just a little too rich for my blood. I headed back home shortly after but I certainly did enjoy the morning.

This afternoon I finally saw what I had so often heard the people talking about. I was downtown and saw two little Cuban girls, no more than six or seven, puffing away on cigarettes. I am told that the kids drink coffee at a very young age here and begin smoking at about the same age. I am beginning to believe more of what I hear every day.

By the way, on the Via Blanca Sunday afternoon I saw for the first time what Cuban speed traps are. I saw two types. The first was just a motorcycle cop pulled off the side of the highway. He had no radar for checking a car's speed but went solely and alone by his judgment. Whenever he thought a car was going too fast, he'd simply jump on his cycle and take off after them. The other type was more fascinating. This consisted of a Crosley Station Wagon with two big conspicuous loudspeakers on top of the car. Trailing behind this station wagon was a motorcycle cop. Inside the station wagon were four men: the driver, the announcer and two license plates or speed spotters. Again, they did not have radar or the like to check the speed of cars. Whenever they thought a car was speeding or saw a driver passing illegally, they would call out the car's license plate over the loudspeaker system (very loud) and tell the driver to pull over. The motorcycle cop would then pull out in front, catch the driver, give him a ticket. No one ever tried outrunning the cop either, not with political conditions as they are. The cops would not shoot for your tires but for the driver, assuming that the driver was a rebel who was trying to escape. It is also surprising how the Cuban drivers help their fellow drivers when a speed trap is ahead. The oncoming traffic will put their headlights on. Of course, if they get caught with their lights on it is too bad for them. However, it serves the purpose. Several times Mr. Herr saw the lights of oncoming traffic go on and he slowed down. Sure enough, a short distance ahead was a motorcycle cop or one of these station wagons.

Not much more news but I guess this is plenty. It at least takes plenty of time to type. I did see where the Braves lost a doubleheader Sunday. They can't afford too many of those but I still think they should be able to take it. There's no doubt that the Cards will give them the roughest time. I haven't seen too many box scores but this boy Hazle seems to be doing ok. Could be that he and Schoendienst are the two men they needed. Perhaps Bruton will have a rough time getting back in the line-up. Talk about messed up box scores in the Havana paper. Sunday's paper had the Yankees winning a doubleheader; one game from Kansas City and the other from the Phillies.

Dave

P.S. Perhaps you can send this letter along to Walt and Bill. That way they will be getting more detailed info on Havana. I just won't have the time to be as detailed in all my letters. I will try and be more detailed in your letters and let you pass them along. After all, I put most of the stuff from my diary in your letters, so you can see that it is impossible for me to do that in all the letters that I write.

Dear Dad and Ma,

I am afraid this letter won't be too long as I've been on the go all week and will finish the week out the same way. Since Pastor Gruell has returned, we've really been on the go.

I was rather disappointed in hearing from Pastor Gruell last Thursday morning that he wanted me to preach on Sunday, the 25th of August, since they had changed their vacation plans. It caught me completely off-guard since I wasn't supposed to preach on that date originally. Therefore, I had to keep my nose to the grindstone.

Last week Friday I finally received my trunk and suit-case. Both of them held up remarkably well but the suit-case took the worst beating since it was full of books. Quite a few of my clothes were dirty simply because the customs inspectors were not careful. I will have to have them washed before wearing them. Otherwise, everything arrived in rather good condition.

Sunday, we had two visitors from Valpo, Indiana. One was Valpo's athletic director's son. I had a nice visit with them. They knew Dick Hinz, since he had arrived in Valpo for his vicarage only two weeks ago.

Practically all-day Monday was spent in running around the city pricing new school buses. The Mission Board has given Pastor Gruell permission to purchase a new school bus for our Christian Day School out at Reparto Marti. He finally ended up today dickering between a Volkswagen and a German-Ford. He bought the Volkswagen. Also, he is pressing the Mission Board to buy a car for my use. He feels rather confident that that Mission Board will give their approval. As a matter of fact, he almost bought a new Renault yesterday on good faith but then he decided he had better wait until he had permission. One thing is for sure, if I'm to do the work he expects of me, I will need a car. The members and mission prospects are just too far and widely scattered.

As soon as I can get them fitted out, I will be living in a couple of the rooms on the second floor of the house where we currently worship. I will have to buy a single bed, mattress, sheets, pillow, towels and wash clothes. I will also need a chest of drawers, a chair, a fan and a refrigerator. The fan and the refrigerator are the two most expensive items. I will be glad to receive my check for the month of August so I can do some buying. My meals I'll eat over at the Pastor's house for the time being ($55.00 a month) and my laundry I'll have done over at the Herr's ($2.00 to $3.00 a week). That should pretty well fix me up. Pastor Gruell told me that he heard I was supposed to get $275.00 a month form the mission board instead of $185.00 per month. Reason for that is that living costs are so high here. He said he'd do all in his power to see that I got it.

Last night we went out on our first calls. Made about five of them, finding only two home. It seems rather odd to first be making calls after 8:30 but that is Cuban life. Their evening doesn't begin until about 8:30 and then lasts until about midnight or 1 a.m. We made calls until about 10:30 when Pastor took sick and just about passed out. I had to drive him home. He's been having head trouble (nervousness) since Sunday. One can readily understand why when you realize the pace this guy sets. Every day we've been on the go from 8:30 until 10:30 to 11:00 a.m. making calls. When he writes his sermons, I don't know and when I'll write mine if I have to keep up this pace, I don't know.

I learned that he is instructing 22 adults at present and they are all individual instructions. He has to go to their homes since it doesn't work to get them together for a class. I'm supposed to inherit about half or more of these instructions. For this reason alone, a car is a necessity because these people live in all four corners and outlying suburbs of Havana. It's a real rat race!!!

Today is Pastor's birthday and I'm invited over to his place for supper tonight. I haven't had time to get him anything as yet and prospects don't look too good. He'll be calling on me in about an hour. After 7:00 supper, we are going out calling again. We have to see this refugee family and then make a few other calls. I had hoped to begin work on my sermon for September 8th by this time but just no time. Get up at 6:30-6:45, wash, eat breakfast, have my devotion and Scripture reading, get over to church and go out on calls. Time; time; time---where is it?

By the way, the address you have been sending the letters to is correct. Miramar is a suburb of Havana like Wauwatosa is of Milwaukee. La Puntilla is part of Miramar where, if you remember, I told you the Rio Almendares enters Havana. La Puntilla means point, and it is on the point of the Almendares River in Miramar where Pastor Gruell lives. Just to refresh your memory.

Did you see in the paper where Hazle was hitting .526 for the Braves? Had no idea he was over .500 but I figured from the few box scores I had seen that he was hitting a rather torrid pace. They sure can use a hitter like that, especially when Aaron is in a slump. Believe the Braves have it now. All they have to do is play steady ball. Too bad I can't see the Series.

I hope to be in the States sometime in October with Pastor Gruell for the Georgia-Florida winter conference. Also, next April, I will again be in the States for a conference. Pastor Gruell said I'm to go along with him for both. Will feel good to set foot on U.S. soil again.

Dave

P.S. Heard from Walt last week but haven't had time to answer him yet. Must try and keep pace with Pastor Gruell first and then take care of letter writing.

2

SEPTEMBER 1957

La Habana, Cuba
September 8, 1957

Dear Dad and Ma,

Finally, I'm about settled in my own living quarters. I moved into one of the rooms above the church this past week. About all that remains to be done is to get my trunk over here and unpack it.

Was more or less behind the eight ball this past week when it came to letter writing as you have already discovered. Of course, my first case of tropical dysentery didn't help matters. I came down with it late Saturday evening and it carried over through Tuesday morning. I was in bed most of the time except for Sunday services and Bible Class. The severe cramps are really incapacitating.

Last Tuesday I attended my first Cuban funeral. To put it mildly, I was rather disappointed. In the first place, Pastor didn't know he had it until about three hours before the service. (That's one thing about Cubans; they make arrangements on the spur of the moment and they waste no time in burying the dead.) Then, after preaching a wonderful Law/Gospel message to the survivors, one would think that not a word had penetrated their hearts. As the survivors filed passed the coffin for the last viewing, they became hysterical. The women practically went into convulsions and the friends were not much better. Pastor tried to comfort the mother and surviving daughter, but it was to no avail. The way they carried on one would certainly think the devil had possession of them. I thought the mother would die of a heart attack. This went on for about 20 minutes or longer until they finally loaded the casket in the hearse.

Also, the actions of the people working in the mortuary were horrible. They paid no respect for the deceased person but walked through the room smoking their cigars in their dirty old clothes, making no attempt to keep quiet. People (workers and who knows who else) were tramping in and out all the time.

What really took the cake, though, was the committal service. Two workers carried the casket to the grave and then lowered it down by means of cattle rope. Then, before Pastor even had an opportunity to begin the committal service, two workingmen began shoveling the dirt into the hole. They continued this throughout the entire service and nearly had the hole filled by the time the pastor finished. Pastor was standing to the side of the grave and the husband was standing alongside it all by himself. One worker was on each side of him, so the husband was in the center as they filled in the hole. You can imagine about how he felt. And he showed it shortly after they had finished with their work. It was the first time he broke down, which I considered very good considering the way the others carried on.

As far as I am concerned, this is just one of those things you have to see to believe. And it isn't very pleasant to see them. It takes away all the joy of knowing that another believer in Jesus has gone home to heaven. Instead, you'd think that there was no eternal life in heaven after death; that the person had most certainly gone to hell. The shouting, screaming, and hollering is deafening and very sickening.

Everything was made up for the funeral, though, on Tuesday. Tuesday evening, I went with the pastor as he instructed a Cuban family. They were very pleasant people, very much interested in our church and very well acquainted with their Bibles. No doubt they would put many a good Lutheran of long standing to shame the way they could flip through their Bibles and find the passages. At any rate, attending such a class you can well see what St. Paul means when he says that there is no distinction between people of all nations; that the Gospel is meant for all. I can well understand why Pastor Gruell likes his work here so well. This type of work just grows and grows on a person.

Friday evening, I conducted my first service at Hershey's mission station. It's about a two-hour ride from Havana but very beautiful and scenic. If only I had a 35 mm. camera, I could take plenty of colored slides. As a matter of fact, I may pick one up in Miami when we come over for the Fla.-Ga. convention in October. The investment would well be worth it. Getting back to Hershey. We eat supper every Friday night at the Anderson's, in whose house we have our worship service in their living room. They are a Jamaican family, in their fifties, coal black but just as good hearted as can be. She is a tremendous cook---always has arroz con pollo and plenty else to eat. He is a very nice fellow and well versed in the Bible also. Their house is spotlessly clean, as are most of the colored people's homes. As a matter of fact, I would say they keep cleaner homes than many American homes. It is a pleasure to sit and visit with them in their homes. It is a great blessing and privilege to be able to bring them the Word of God. There are only about ten members but they show up practically 100% every Friday evening. I do believe that my Friday evening services at Hershey will be one of the high spots of my vicarage.

Starting October, Pastor wants to begin a Saturday School from 9-12 noon. I'll have charge of the English children and he'll take the Spanish. We'll take turns picking the children up in the school bus (Volkswagen) which during the week is used out at our Christian Day School at Reparto Marti. About the only way you can make such a thing a success is to go out and pick up the children. They are spread over too wide a territory to expect them to come via their own transportation.

This week, unless we hear from the Mission Board tomorrow, I'll be without transportation. Last week I was able to use the new Volkswagen bus which they had just bought but since school starts tomorrow that means of transportation is out. Nothing at all to driving the bus and it really handles nicely. Top speed is 80 kilometers. The whining motor does sort of get on your nerves but you have to put up with it for economy's sake. It parks easily. I could park it places that Dad could never get his DeSoto in. Well, we will wait and see what the Mission Board says. Pastor Gruell wants them to get me a Renault.

By the way, I don't feel badly about not writing last week as I also failed to hear from you. Yesterday I received five letters but yours was not with them. I had one from Wally & Olga, Pearl, Wib (my roommate last year), the vicar at the Isle of Pines and the Mission Board.

Also, if I remember correctly, Ma said something about rates being cheaper at Christmas. However, as I told you previously, send nothing, nothing, nothing, nothing, nothing, nothing! Nothing that is sent into Cuba is cheaper at any time, not even at Christmas. The duty I would have to pay

21

on it would be much more than the package itself is worth. For example, Pastor's parents thought the same as Ma and sent him several $1.00 pair of socks. He had to pay over $4.00 duty on three pair of socks. See what I mean. It just doesn't pay. And never send money. It would not get through the post office here. I am told that too many of their employees have sticky fingers.

This morning we had one present at the Spanish service. That was me. At the English service we had between 40-45, which is exceptional. Also had about 10 in Bible Class which is very good. Pastor was out of Havana today. He had to go down to the Isle of Pines for communion services while their pastor is on his six-month vacation in the States. Pastor Gruell returns tomorrow morning.

Guess I'll have to cut this short now. I have several other letters to write yet. Don't get too much time because I leave about 9:00 a.m. and am kept busy enough until about 11:00 p.m. every day. It's fascinating work but with this humidity and heat it is also a very tiring pace.

Dave

House in Havana rented by Trinity Lutheran Church for worship.
Sunday School rooms and Vicar Dissen's living quarters were upstairs.
The church office was in a back room on the ground floor.

Dear Dad and Ma,

Friday evening Pastor Gruell received word from the Mission Board to "go" ahead and buy a Renault. At the time, I was in Hershey conducting the regular Friday evening services. When I returned about 11:00 at night, I saw the Renault standing out in front of Pastor's apartment. It's really a nice little job. A dark blue sportsman's model. It now has white sidewalls on it but they will be taken off tomorrow. For economy, you can't beat it. It is supposed to get 70 kilometers (about 42 miles) to the gallon. You sort of have to roll yourself up to get into it. The Cubans seem to get a bang out of watching me unwind myself when I get out, for when I stand alongside it, I'm am quite a bit taller than it.

The past week we visited a new family that had just moved to Havana from Mexico City. Last name was Hedin. As it turned out, Mr. Hedin (about 28) is from Rolette, North Dakota and is a first cousin to the Hedin's of New Rockford where Dad had been pastor. We had plenty about which to talk. Only thing is, he is a Mason. That means a little work ahead of me. Pastor figures, though, that maybe since we have common North Dakota backgrounds I may have somewhat of an opening whereby I can work with him. I sure hope so. They are a very nice young couple.

As of now, I am instructing three adults separately at their homes on Tuesdays. First instruction is at 9:30 and the last one at 3:30 in the afternoon. Perhaps I will soon be able to add one or two more adults to instruction.

I met several very interesting families this past week who are under my English Communicant list. How they ever got on that list is beyond me. One family has no time for church at all on Sundays and appears to be way off the beam religiously, very close to naturalists. The other woman is an avowed pantheist and naturalist. She does not believe in sin; the O.T.; very little of the N.T.; no belief in the true God; and no belief in her Savior. She believes that Mohammed is just as good as Jesus and is a stronger advocate of the Koran then the Bible. It really rends one's heart to see people who are supposedly Lutheran make such confessions. Naturally, unless God graciously opens their eyes and makes them see their errors they will soon be disciplined. We do not know who was responsible for their acceptance as communicant members. Pastor Gruell wasn't. Perhaps it's best for all concerned that no one ever finds out. But Christian discipline will have to be taken unless their belief changes.

Friday evening, I went out to Hershey by myself. I had only three hours in which to get ready. The pastor who was to conduct service that night became ill and couldn't go. I was unprepared but went anyway. I used an old sermon but had to refer to the manuscript several times. First time I ever did this.

How I wish I had a 35mm. color camera when I take this trip out to Hershey. Believe me, the scenery is simply gorgeous and breath-taking. Especially when you travel alongside the ocean and later when you get more into the interior mountains. Perhaps in several months I can afford a good camera and then get some pictures for slides that are worth taking and keeping.

This week, now that I have my own transportation, Pastor is letting me on my own. The days are mine and I set up my own schedule. I am glad in a way, because now maybe I can devote more time to my sermon preparation once again. The three weeks pastor has been back we've been so busy making calls that sermon preparation suffered quite heavily.

It could be that by the first of the year we'll be breaking ground for our Church in Havana. At the same time pastor received the "green light" for the Renault, he was also told to get several lots ready for the mission board representatives when they come down here. They will probably be here in a week or sooner. They also want him to pick out a house for his family. Could be that this will be a big year all the way around for Havana. A new church, a parsonage, and a Saturday school. All should advance the cause of the Kingdom.

Pastor told me that if I'd like to, he'd be willing to give me the third weekend in October off so I could go down to the Isle of Pines and visit the vicar who is down there. The expense will be my own but the round-trip plane fare is only $12.75. I may take him up on it. It would be a good opportunity to relax a little and get away from this nerve-wrecking pace of a big city.

24

I bought two pair of slacks last week and several bow ties. Next is white shirts. Believe me, this weather is very hard on clothes. White shirts you can't wear more than half a day if you want them looking anywhere decent. Just too much humidity and heat. Same for the regular ties. You wear them once or twice and they become so creased they look terrible. Bow ties are about the only answer. Slacks you can hardly wear more than three times and then it's the cleaners.

This past week Pastor and I had our first game of wiffle ball. One of his son's found the wiffle balls they had bought in the states on their vacation under the back seat of his car. Pastor really goes for the game, really eats it up. That'll be one means of relaxation we'll have together. Also last Monday I went golfing for the first time in my life with the Pastor Gruell. Aside from one good drive, I managed to dig up a lot of Cuban ground. I missed a par on the 5th hole by one stroke. Obviously, I didn't do very good. It could be that golf isn't my game.

I had expected the Braves to show a few signs of nervousness, but they'd better snap out of it. Time is fast running out and this isn't the time to go on a long losing streak. I hope Spahn brings them out of it today and puts them back in winning ways. I must begin work on my sermon for next Sunday today so will close for now. Much work to do and not much time to write long letters anymore.

Dave

Dear Dad and Ma,

I will try and get a start on this letter yet tonight. I have been working on my sermon for Sunday all day so this will be a welcome change and a chance for a breather.

Talking about breathers, I had a very pleasant one Sunday (yesterday) afternoon. I went along with Pastor Gruell's family to Jibacoa. Jibacoa is a private, very exclusive settlement about 40 miles out of Havana, situated on the coastline with several very nice beaches. Pastor had a guest card from one of the families living there, so we were permitted to enter. It was my first-time swimming here. Also, my first swim ever in the Atlantic Ocean. Really a lot of fun, especially when the big breakers come rolling in. They are strong enough to pull your feet right out from under you. The water is slightly saltier than a swimming pool would be and also a little dirtier. After we went swimming, the family whose guests we were, took us on a sightseeing trip of the territory. Really very beautiful views. Too bad I didn't have my camera along with color film. All in all, it was a very enjoyable day. Didn't have any trouble sleeping last night.

Friday night Pastor, his wife and I took in a Jai-Alai game. The first time for all of us. It's a very interesting game and very fast. Much depends upon wrist action and a set body position. I got one of the ushers to bring a Jai-Alai ball and basket up to us. Believe me, that ball is much harder than a baseball. The basket is woven and is strapped onto the wrist. A little heavier than I thought it would be. You need good, strong wrists; quick re-action and much vigor to play the game. How they can ever follow the ball all the time is beyond me. I surely wouldn't want to get hit in the head by one of those balls that's in motion. I don't think you'd have much of a chance for survival. That's why they have the entire playing court entirely screened off.

We had the news from the Mission Board that they will be down here a week from today to look at lots for a church and a parsonage. I was also told that my salary adjustment was approved, and I would be receiving $275.00 per month. Sounds like a lot of money but expenses are quite a bit higher here than in the States. Clothes alone are a big item. The heat and

26

humidity make it necessary for two changes a day at least. Suits and pants after one wearing usually look as if you've slept in them all night. I'll welcome the adjustment, just as will the vicar on the Isle of Pines. He also knows what it costs.

The little Renault has really been getting a good workout. We haven't had it a week yet (take that back, it's a week and a half we've had it) and already we have 800 some kilometers on it. Surely does the trick, though. It's very economical and a real gem in heavy traffic and parking situations.

Tomorrow is instruction day again, so my day will be pretty well taken up. That means Wednesday before I get an opportunity to write out my sermon. With calls and other tasks, my time is well taken. Last week, I averaged about 5 calls per day. Won't keep that pace up always because it takes too much time from my sermon preparation. I had a talk with Pastor last Saturday afternoon and he said he would back me 100% in putting my sermon first. I was more or less getting the idea he wanted me out making calls most of the time. As a result, my sermons were suffering, and I was frustrated. He was very understanding about the whole thing, which makes it much easier.

Friday I'll be going out to Hershey again. Looks more and more as if that will also be my responsibility. I don't mind it one bit though as it's a tremendous experience. Also, a beautiful drive that I'll never tire of seeing.

Go Braves! They're much closer now than a week ago. Two wins from the Cards will give it to them. Would like to be in Milwaukee if and when they clinch it. Wow! The Braves will really do a war dance, with all the other celebrations. Bedlam will literally break loose. I was glad to see Spahn nail down his 20th win. Now, I would like to see Buhl do the same. I didn't realize that he has nine consecutive victories going for him. At least that's what the Havana papers say.

I hope to see Dad on television at Milwaukee Stadium for at least one of the games. I understand that they are televised to Cuba. Pastor has a TV set, so we'll be all set for the Series. He, too, is a rabid Milwaukee fan. You can guess what we talk about in our spare moments.

Dave

La Habana, Cuba
September 30, 1957

Dear Dad and Ma,

I finally did hear from Bill and Marilyn last Saturday. I was more or less giving up hopes of ever hearing from them. She did state in her letter that she had inquired at the Post Office and they told her only $.08 was needed for an Air Mail letter to Cuba but it didn't work. As a result, I ended up getting their letter which was written on August 23 and mailed on the 24th on the 28th of September. That's what you would call very fast "pony express." Naturally it was nice hearing from them but they may as well spend the $.02 extra and speed things up a bit.

Last week was a rather busy one for me. On Thursday I went with pastor to Boca de Galafre, a short distance from Pinar del Rio. This is on the southern end of Cuba, about 240 kilometers from Havana. About a 4-hour drive one way. We took the little Renault and it really handled like a gem on the highway.

Of course, the drive was very beautiful. Especially the mountains in the background, with the Palm trees making a very impressive foreground. Saw the Caribbean Sea for the first time as Boca de Galafre is only ½ a mile from the Caribbean.

It is down in the Southern part of the Island that political conditions are the worst. We felt it in two ways while down there. In the first place, open public gatherings were prohibited so we held services (Spanish) in the thatched roof house of the only Lutheran family there instead of the regular town hall. Services were at 7:30 in the evening and we had a nice turn out (45 present). Of course, if you want to get a real picture of the environment of the services here it is like this, with chairs placed in the living room and dining room of the house, making an L shape nave with the makeshift altar and pulpit at the base of the L. There is no electricity in the house but instead four oil lanterns used for light (very poor light); no piano or organ but singing of hymns led by the Lutheran wife of the family. Probably a little more or less like St. Paul in the N.T. but it was still very edifying, spiritually. Since the rebels had been burning all places where people gathered publicly (or bombing them), including R.C. Churches, I was stationed at the front door to watch for any signs of trouble. Everything went off fine as we had figured, for our arrival and the announcement of services was on very short notice. We figured that by the time the rebels did plan anything if they did get wind of our conducting services, we would be through by then.

Home of a Lutheran family in Boca de Galafre, where worship services were held. Most of the time the people stood for the entire service so that everyone could crowd into the house. Pastor Gruell and I would try to arrive there by noon, eat lunch, take a siesta, then go up the mountains to the tobacco sheds to invite people to worship. After eating we sat outside to watch the people descend the mountains in small groups, heading to worship.

Our second experience almost turned out the worst. It was on our way back to Havana after services. We left about 9:00 at night. I was driving. While heading out of Pinar del Rio, I noticed a group of soldiers with guns at their sides stationed alongside the highway. Of course, I had heard of the frequent inspections they made of cars, just for security measures. However, I figured if they wanted me to stop, they'd flag me down. Therefore, I put the car into second and slowed down to a crawl. I drew even with them and still no signal to stop so I started stepping on the gas. It was just the thing I shouldn't have done. Luckily, I was still partially watching the soldiers as I began to pass them. As I stepped on the gas, I just caught a glimpse of them raising their rifles to fire. Pastor also saw it and sitting closest to them (first in line of fire) he about jumped out of the car trying to get me to stop. Believe me, I wasted no time in stopping! The soldiers came over to the car, whipped the doors open and gave us a good scolding. However, Pastor explained to them in his very good Spanish that I was new here and didn't quite know the exact political situation. They then motioned us on. It was then that Pastor warned me to stop whenever there were soldiers stationed along the highway.

He said they never flag you down but they take it for granted that you know they want you to stop. And if you don't, they get in a little live rifle practice. There's no doubt we had the guardian angels with us that night, for we came mighty close to death. Of course, as I said, most of the trouble is down in the southern part of the island. There isn't nearly as much worry here in Havana.

Friday morning was spent in the hospital with Mr. Hedin, one of our prospects about whom I told you in my last letter. He's the cousin of the Hedin's in New Rockford and also hails from N.D. He was hit by a car in Havana while crossing the street and very seriously and painfully injured. It happened Wednesday and we didn't get the news until Thursday. Of course, by that time we had already left for Boca de Galafre and were gone all day. As a result, we were first able to call on him Friday. I was with him until about half an hour before he went into the operating room. Then pastor relieved me. Mr. Hedin had to have a pin put in his left leg. Naturally, he was in much pain yet Saturday when I went to see him but he was feeling much better yesterday. He seems to be taking it much better now. They are a very swell couple and we hope to instruct them soon. He is Swedish Lutheran and she is Presbyterian but they both want to join our church. Of course, we have the lodge problem with him.

Friday afternoon and evening were spent in Hershey, so all day Friday was also taken up. This pace keeps one going but I wouldn't give it up for anything. At times it gets a little nervy but then that's life wherever you go.

Must get cleaned up and go out to the airport. In about an hour, two members from the Mission Board are to arrive. We trust that they will give us the "green light" on building a church and a parsonage.

Go you Braves!! I'll be watching the first game on TV and as many as possible thereafter. I sure hope they take it. By the way, let me know when Dad goes to the hospital for sure, okay!

Dave

3

OCTOBER 1957

La Habana, Cuba
October 6, 1957

Dear Dad and Ma,

Just came back to my room from Pastor Gruell's after watching this afternoon's Series' game. Believe me, my blood pressure was running high in the 9th inning when Haney let Spahn stay in and then Howard belted him for a game tying homer. It was very obvious that Spahn did not have it in this inning for all his pitches were coming in high. That is a very plain signal that Spahn is tired but Haney blinded himself to the fact. Instead, he pats Spahn on the seat and says, in effect, "That's all right Spahn, you're a nice fella and I want you to have a chance to win at least one game!" So far as I am concerned, that's not managing at all. Instead, it's letting personality play too much into the picture. After all, does one man make the team or do nine? I must admire Casey for the way he handles his men. It's obvious that he's all baseball right down to the wire. There's no "nice guy" personality in him that's going to let a pitcher stay in when he doesn't have it. He's solid baseball and he's out to win.

Well, all this griping for nothing since the Braves did win in the 10th on the strength of Matthews clout. I do believe that Eddie's Homer pulled Haney out of the fire, though. His (Haney's) tactics are utterly ridiculous. Though the Braves did get clobbered yesterday, they still fought back "bravely" today. Now that they had to come from behind to win, maybe it'll perk them up and motivate them to win. I'm pulling for them all the way. Of course, Pastor Gruell is a Yankee fan, so we have a fun time watching the Series.

I am praying that Dad's operation turns out well and that he's back on his feet soon. It's hard to keep him down, so I don't envy the nurses one bit. Just hope the Braves have the series clinched by then. It'll make him rest much more comfortably. Hope to send him a card the early part of this week if I can find a decent one. That's a real problem here in Havana. They have a very poor selection of cards.

This past week turned out to be rather profitable for the church's

31

future in Havana. The Mission Board representatives were here and they okayed the purchase of lots for a church and a parsonage. Both lots have been bought so all that remains is the ground-breaking and building. Pastor Ott left Friday for the States and the Dorre's left Saturday. As a result, Monday through Friday was spent mainly with them. However, we are well satisfied with the results.

Yesterday was the first day of Saturday School. Really turned out swell. It was my first experience as a bus driver. Left on my run at 7:15 a.m. and arrived back at church at 8:50 a.m. I was glad to get back because it was mostly city driving. And city driving with a bus load of antsy children about wears on your nerves. We had nineteen in all that turned out for the first day of class. Of those, I had nine in my class. The remainder were split with three teachers.

I now know what I'll be doing Saturday mornings but it is well worth it. I believe that a Saturday School should be a tremendous help in building the future. The children were really enthused about it. They thought it should last longer than three hours. Can you believe that? That in itself is quite an admission for kids to make. Right, Dad and Ma? Even Eunice,[1] as a school teacher, should know that.

By the way, how's the school teacher doing? Have you been able to quiet down the thundering herds? Or do you have all "sweet little angels" in your class?

Will have to finish this letter later. Pastor and I have a luncheon appointment at 5:30 so I better get cleaned up. Just had to sit down and start writing, though, after Matthews treated me to that 10th inning dessert with his home-run.

Am back at the typewriter again, only much later than I had figured. Here it is, Monday morning (or I should say noon). I have a few minutes before leaving for dinner, so will finish this pronto.

Yesterday afternoon Pastor was informed that we have our Pastoral conference in Miami from Tuesday noon to Thursday noon of this week. Therefore, we've been more than busy in order to have everything in shape so we can leave by plane tomorrow morning. Hope to call you Wednesday evening or so if it isn't too expensive. I will also be able to pick up a card for

---

[1] My sister, Eunice Dissen, lived with Dad and Ma during school vacations. There were six children in our family (some mentioned in other letters): William, Walter, David (myself), Eunice, Martin, and Fred.

Dad, I hope.

This past week we had plenty of rain in Havana. Their drainage is very poor and as a result many of the lower places are flooded out. I had to sit and wait in one place over an hour before I could go two blocks. It was at a low point and the water was two to three feet deep. The Renault may have plenty of advantages but it cannot plow through water like a bigger car. It's just too small. Chances are the water would have turned the car over the way it was gushing over the curb. About two more weeks and the rain should be over for three or four months. Then we have the nicest season of the year in Havana.

They're after me to teach English out at our Spanish Christian Day School again. I don't think I'll do it since it would be a commitment until next June. That's too much of an obligation so far as I'm concerned. I'll have my hands full enough without teaching English.

It's probably best if you wait with paying Walt his $65.00 until December (the first or thereabouts). Perhaps about that time he'd appreciate it more.

Will get some of those recipes from Mrs. Gruell one of these days. Believe me, she's a real good cook and has some dandies. Only thing is, I don't know if you can get the same kind of fruits and vegetable in the States as we do here. Fried bananas are a green banana, different than the yellow eating banana you get in Union Grove.

Dave

P.S. Can't Dad sabotage the Yanks some way or another?! They're close enough that he should be able to do something. Of course, the Braves don't really need that kind of help but Dad could throw a scare into those "Yankees."

Dear Dad and Ma, and Eunice,

Well, we arrived back in Havana Friday evening about 5:00 p.m. I'd be a liar if I didn't say it was nice to set foot in the U.S. again. I will admit, though, that many things seemed somewhat strange. I guess it doesn't take too long to get accustomed to a different culture as I've only been over here about 2 ½ months.

I enjoyed talking to Ma and Eunice but perhaps I'd better not call anymore if Ma always reacts the way she did. She gets so excited and then right away thinks that something is wrong. Of course, Dad is the same way. It seems every time I call that you think something is wrong. Maybe I should stick to letters, huh?

I really had my work cut out for me when I got back. I was able to get very little studying done in Miami so I had it all to do when we reached Havana. Friday evening, we were invited out to a big supper at one of the members in honor of their parents, who were visiting from the States. After that, Pastor and I had to mimeograph the material for Saturday School. Then Saturday morning was taken up with Saturday School. That left me the grand total of Saturday afternoon and evening to really study. I did manage all right Sunday morning but I don't believe I'd care for that kind of pressure with every sermon.

The conference went very swell. We had a good turn out every day from Tuesday through Thursday. Prof. Rehwinkel was the essayist. He was just like he is in the classroom at the Seminary. He has a good mind and good material but at times he gets a little absent minded and wanders in his thoughts. As a result, we had several good laughs. One for instance was this: He was intent upon telling the pastors how much he appreciated the Florida hospitality and the opportunity to be with them so he said: "Brothers, I certainly enjoy this wonderful 'California' sunshine and the privilege to serve you at this conference." Of course, the California comment brought down the rafters with laughter (and a few boos were also mixed in). Our next conference is in April, so I imagine that is the next time I'll be in Florida. And by the way, don't get overly excited if you should get another phone call about that time.

On our way up to the States, we flew over to Key West and then rode up via car with the pastor from key West, Pastor Carl Sammetinger. Naturally we had to take the Overseas Highway. This is really a beautiful drive. Most of the way you have miles and miles of ocean water on both sides of the highway. One bridge in itself is a masterpiece of engineering, stretching over seven miles of water. Thus, it is referred to as the Seven Mile Bridge. One evening we took a drive along the hotel section. Boy, you should see some of the fabulous hotels they have in Miami. No wonder it is such a popular vacation spot.

The apartment in which we stayed was situated right on the Ocean. I forgot my swimming trunks so it did me no good. One thing that impressed me was the abundance of natural sand beaches. While we have plenty of water around us in Cuba, there are only about two natural sand beaches. The rest are all coral.

Lest I be anathematized, I should by all means mention that we faithfully watched the World Series while in attendance at the conference. The conference made a motion to meet from 2:30 to 5:30 on Wednesday and Thursday instead of from 1:30 to 4:30. This, thereby, gave us an opportunity to watch the last two games.

While Buhl pitched way below par, Burdette really picked up the slack. I wouldn't be one bit surprised if he could be elected Mayor of Milwaukee on account of his brilliant performances. What a "gem" that guy turned out to be. He was simply F A B U L O U S! And Matthews, Schoendienst, Covington and Johnson also deserve a big hand. I'll bet Wisconsin is delighted, now that the World Champs are residing there. So much for the Braves. It is now history but joy resigns supreme in BRAVES-LAND.

Yesterday afternoon I had nothing to do so in what better way could I spend my time than looking for Gran Stadium, the home of winter baseball in Havana. I had the good fortune of finding it in good time and to my amazement a game was in progress. (Now who would ever have thought that I knew a game was being played, let alone a doubleheader?) Naturally, I couldn't pass by a ball park when they were playing so I bought a ticket

($1.40) and enjoyed the doubleheader. I saw Manager Bobby Bragan, Loyd Merritt (Cards), Ramon Mejias, Willie Miranda, Rocky Nelson, Clyde McCullough and Harry Chiti to name a few. Merritt looked rather good even though he was losing 2-1 in the seventh inning of the second game when I left. He was using a Don Larsen, no wind-up pitch. Aside from the Major Leaguers playing, most of the others looked strictly like bush leaguers. Several bad plays were made that you'd rarely see in the Majors.

Took my first roll of pictures the other week and hope to bring them in for development sometime this week. If they turn out good, I'll send you some. They are all scenic shots of Cuba. One was taken in Miami at our apartments but that is the only Stateside picture.

This week I'll really have to brush up on my Spanish. Pastor wants me to conduct my first Altar Service in Spanish. I'll give it a try but it's going to be far from perfect.

Dave

P.S. I hope Dad is feeling much better now. Also hope that he got to see his Braves clinch the series on Thursday afternoon. If I know him, the first thing he asked Ma Wednesday when he came out of the anesthetic was "What did the Braves do?"

October 22, 1957
La Habana, Cuba

Dear Dad and Ma,

Had one big goose-egg for all my chasing around this morning as both of my adult class attendees that I have on Tuesday morning were either ill or absent. Thus, this morning was shot in which I could have put in more time on my sermon for Sunday. As yet I do not have a good start on it.

Was glad to receive the "Special Braves Edition," even though I didn't receive your letter last week. It first arrived yesterday, along with the newspaper.

The old North Wind is beginning to blow and will continue to do so for about three months. It really whips up the ocean. Yesterday evening before supper, I was standing on the Gruell's patio watching the waves breaking off the shore. Many of them were like little geysers, shooting 25 feet or more into the air. They tell me that when the wind really blows the waves reach as high as 50 and 75 feet. I will be looking forward to that.

Am still awaiting the return of my first roll of film. Not any pictures on it that would interest you but I'm merely interested in seeing what kind of job they do on them. The next roll I have in the camera contains mainly shots on the way to Hershey. Very scenic. If they turn out, I'll send a few.

Last Sunday I conducted my first Spanish altar service. It was far from perfect from the language point of view but then one has to wade in and give it a try some time. At least my feet are now wet.

I have seen two Havana league baseball games already. Naturally it was against my will to go since I don't care for the game. Yet, it's funny how you can become attached to something that you don't like so quickly. It's a good thing I didn't have the baseball bug in Wisconsin or I'd probably have gone to see the Braves also.

Last week I had what will eventually be a "Round Robin" letter for about six of us who are out on vicarage this year. Three of them had written and sent their letters onto me. I was the fourth, Gene Wille makes the fifth and my roommate makes the sixth. It sort of runs into postage for me by the time it gets here and I then have to send it on.

I heard from both Winnie and Uncle Charlie last week also. I've now written to just about everyone once. It seems as if I have Fred and Mart left but no addresses for them. I take that back. I do have Fred's address.

Not much more to say. Too much work to write anymore.

Dave

October 28, 1957
La Habana, Cuba

Dear Dad and Ma, and Eunice,

Old Man North Wind has really been stirring up a fuss the last two days and is still at it today. The temperatures have dropped down to the freezing point of about 70°! Freezing, did I say? At least that is what you would think by observing the dress of the Cubans. The policemen yesterday were huddled in every corner, nook and cranny they could find. And they were wearing gloves and heavy wool coats. Everyone seemed to be running around with coats on and also sweaters. It seemed as if I was the only one enjoying the ideal weather and temperature.

This is the season of the year when those people who live alongside the Ocean wish they were a little further inland. The wind sends a fine, misting salt spray flying through the air that rusts out many things. Yesterday was the first day that I really noticed it (the salt spray, that is). Pastor Gruell lives only about ¾ of a block from the Ocean, so they are now suffering from the salt spray. It's terrible stuff, believe me. It gets on everything and you just can't get it off unless you give it a thorough washing.

Yesterday afternoon I was down on the Male Con drive, which is the main drive alongside the Ocean. I had to keep all windows shut on the car because of the waves. They hit the brick wall and then come sloshing up over onto the road. It's almost like being hit with a small cloudburst when one of those waves hits your car. And you can imagine what a mess your car is afterwards. The salt sticks to your windows and makes visibility very poor. It also sticks to the finish of the car and unless you clean the car every day the metal will soon rust out on you. The waves also toss quite a bit of trash up onto the Male Con. There were several places yesterday where one side of the four-lane drive was completely blocked by the trash, mainly wood, large stones etc.

Talking about temperatures, I happened to see in the paper that Chicago had its first snowfall of the year. What a shame! Go South young man! Go South. Visit the sunny, mild clime of Havana. Wear sport shirts the year round and toss away those old red flannels.

Last week we made our monthly trip to Boca de Galafre. This time we took the Ford instead of the Renault. It gave us more space in which to stretch out and also a little more peace of mind. Not quite as much noise from the motor. On our return trip in the evening, I had my eyes open---watching for the armed soldiers. This time I spotted them, even though they were at a different place (and much more inconspicuous). I stopped in plenty of time. Pastor was sleeping but woke up when I had to break to a fast stop. After a couple minutes, we were on our way.

Also, on this last trip to Boca de Galafre we saw quite a bit of fireworks. That is, we saw several fires. I am talking about tobacco sheds that had been set on fire by the rebels. We had just finished eating supper at the Picos's home when I happened to look outside and saw the sky lighting up. That was the first tobacco shed (full of tobacco as were the others) to be torched that night. We left for Havana about 10 minutes later and on the way saw about five more that had been torched. According to Mrs. Picos, in one night alone they set fire to 17 tobacco sheds. That's a big financial loss for the owners.

Yesterday morning we had an Evangelical Congregational Pastor and his wife visit us in our Spanish service. I had to go down to the hotel and bring them out. As a matter of fact, we've had quite a few visiting tourists attend our services who are not members of a Lutheran church.

Well, it's about that time for making some calls this morning so will sign off. I did hear from Bill and Marilyn. Again, Marilyn failed to put enough postage on the letter and as a result her letter written on October 2nd didn't arrive here until October 26th.

Danny McDevitt, Brooklyn's star rookie pitcher, was brutally assaulted by one of the Cuban umpires in the second game of this past Saturday's doubleheader. They took him off the field on a stretcher and his condition is still "serious." He was badly beaten about the head. The police had to break up the riot that followed. Just what caused the fracas, I don't know. Regardless of what it was, that umpire should be suspended for life. Such action is entirely out of place for any umpire.

Dave

4

NOVEMBER 1957

La Habana, Cuba
November 4, 1957

Dear Dad and Ma, and Eunice,

This afternoon the churches of Havana met at the Episcopal Church to discuss the case of the Renelt family. This is the refugee family that I first encountered the latter part of August. Seems as if they have been playing both ends against the middle and receiving charity from many sources. As a result, the churches have been overlapping in their charitable contributions to the family. The purpose of the meeting was to work cooperatively on this case and give them only what they needed. Their first four months in Havana they received about $1,300 in charity. Now you know as well as I do, that is living like kings, especially since the average Cuban working family has a salary of about $125.00 to $150.00 per month. Evidently the Renelt's have been stashing the money away for a "rainy day" when they get their passports into the U.S.

Pastor and I were delegated to talk to the family, present the facts to them, and deal with them spiritually. The main reason for this is that they have been coming to our church and the others felt we were best qualified to handle this spiritual matter. It is a matter of lying and honorableness. Actually, they were primarily guilty of withholding information. They just kept accepting and accepting money, never telling people that they were receiving help from other sources. Seems as if the Catholics alone gave them over $1,000 in help. Secondly came our church and then the Episcopal, Methodist, and Baptist.

Last week was a week for calls since I didn't have to preach last Sunday. Believe me, it seemed as if I hit all the German families at the wrong time. Practically every family let me know what their gripes and complaints were. They gave all kinds of invalid excuses for not coming to church. One of the main reasons was the fact that there were no German services. And this they couldn't stomach at all since they said that Luther was German and therefore God's Word should be preached in German. I'll tell you one thing, when they mentioned that the Word should be preached in German, I ruffled a few feathers. I said in a tactful but clear way that from what I knew about Luther, I doubted it very much if he himself would agree with them. Some of these German members do present a real challenge.

Also last week I begin instructions (adult) with a young couple who have been attending our church regularly for quite some time. She is American Lutheran and he was raised Missouri Synod Lutheran but never confirmed. We were in hopes of being able to accept them on a confession of faith after I had gone through the main doctrines of our Church with them. However, these ideas were rudely shattered. They need an entire, thorough course in Christian Doctrine.

It was really discouraging to see them reveal such an erroneous concept of Christianity. We spent 3 ½ hours the first night mostly discussing two or three issues. One was the possibility of salvation for those who never hear the Word of God, which he thought was entirely possible; another the possibility of salvation by mere faith in a God; and thirdly the doctrine of Baptism. I reckon at the end of the night (11:30) he still was not convinced on the first two points for yesterday after Church he asked pastor about the same two questions. Pastor told me that he gave this man the exact answers I did (Pastor and I discussed this thing the morning after I had the instruction class with him, so he knew what I had told him and was aware of this man's beliefs).

All I can say is that when you start discussing such issues with anyone, you'd better stick to God's Word alone. You are sure and certain only as long as you do this. Once you depart from the Bible, people could easily run rings around you and point out that logically God's Word doesn't make sense.

Last Saturday we hit a high in attendance at our Saturday School. We had 25 in church. Soon we hope to be over 30 and finally reach 50 or better. Through Saturday School, Pastor hopes to lay the foundation of a Parochial Day School. It's very encouraging because the children like it and it also gives us an opportunity to contact the German families through the children. This is the only real contact we have with the German families aside from the home visits.

By the way, you can send Walt a check for $70.00 in payment for the typewriter. I haven't heard from him in over two months now. Could be that he's pulling a Bill stunt. If so, he can expect the same treatment from this end of the line. I don't intend to keep writing to those who do not respond.

Heard from Marilyn again last week and as usual her failure to place the sufficient amount of postage on the letter resulted in its arrival about a month later.

Hope you keep out of contact with the Asian flu. I've succeeded so far but how I don't know. Every family I've called on in the past two weeks has had a siege of it. Maybe over-exposure to it is the cure or remedy for immunization. I had better keep my mouth shut, though, as it is time for me to have my monthly attack of dysentery. That, in many ways, is as bad if not worse than Asiatic flu.

Weather in Havana has been beautiful and balmy this past week. It is ideal winter weather. Just warm enough that you aren't taking a bath in perspiration. In other words, pleasantly warm.

Dave

P.S. Tomorrow evening I begin instructions with the Hedin family also. That now means five different families that I instruct separately, (four on Tuesday and one on Wednesday evening). Mr. Hedin, if you recall, is the man who is related to the Hedin's from New Rockford. I will get into the Mason discussion with him, as he is a Mason.

November 10, 1957
La Habana, Cuba

Dear Dad and Ma,

I did not know that we are now in the season of "stamps" in Cuba. It is a Cuban law that from November 1st until February 1st all mail must also have an "anti-tuberculosis" stamp. That means $.14 for every letter instead of the usual $.13 and it also explains why you failed to hear from me last week. You can imagine my surprise last Saturday (yesterday) when I just about opened the letter that I had written you. All along I was thinking it was your letter to me when it was the Post Office returning my letter to you for insufficient postage. I suppose I'll hear from you tomorrow since your letter didn't arrive last week.

Finally, I did hear from Walt. Believe me, he's almost as bad as Bill in letter writing. Still haven't heard from Fred or Mart. I wrote both of them, sending the letter to Fred's address. Perhaps they're too pre-occupied with other things.

It was really a pleasure this morning to have a good organist playing the organ. She is the wife of the American consulate. She will now be our regular organist. She can really make our Hammond "sing." Previously another member and our Pastor's wife had been taking care of the playing. Pastor's wife is good but she just didn't have the time to practice with five young ones to take care of. The other member was slower in her playing than the singing at Fessenden, North Dakota, one of Dad's previous parishes. This morning was almost like listening to Elsie play.

Am aware that today is Luther's birthday as well as the birthday of one of my brothers. Which one I'm not sure but I know it's either Mart or Walt. Will have to try and get downtown tomorrow and pick up some kind of birthday card.

By the way, it did my heart good to see one of our very delinquent church goers in attendance this morning. I had called on her about a month ago. I never thought I would see the day when she would enter the door of our church. I guess I was mistaken. I only wish that more of these "back-sliders" would put in an appearance. We have a communicant list of 84 members on the English rolls. However, I don't believe that more than 35 of them have attended service since I've been here. Thus, you can see the so-called "dead-weight" we're carrying.

Last week we held a meeting in connection with the Renelt family on the point of their charitable relief. We met with all the others in Havana who had been helping them besides our church. Pastor and I were selected as coordinators between the committee and the Renelts. All help is to be channeled through us to the family. Since they had supposedly received about $1300 in relief since arriving in Cuba last June, we had to check into this with the family. It appears that the 3 Catholic women who had been helping them had given them the most. They claimed they gave them over a $1,000 in support. However, we checked with the family and they practically vindicated themselves on every point. Apparently, these women were not happy that this family did not enroll their child in an Augustinian school. Our next committee meeting is this Tuesday evening at 5:00. Pastor intends to make a public apology to all present for even listening to the unkind words spoken against this family. Could turn out to be a rather contentious meeting but I believe Pastor has all the evidence he needs to discount the women's story.

This Sunday Pastor is in the Isle of Pines. I had planned to go down there this afternoon and join him and the vicar in a day's fishing tomorrow. I changed my mind, though, and decided to work on my sermon for next Sunday tomorrow. All day Tuesday is taken up in adult instructions and I hate to lose Mondays when I preach the following Sunday. That means I wouldn't be able to begin my sermon until Wednesday.

The past couple of weeks have really been trying ones out at Hershey. Services are held at 8:00 every Friday evening. It seems as if most of the kids of Hershey hang out around our meeting place. Then when services begin, they start making noise outside the house. They whistle, shout, pound on the windows and building and do practically everything but tear it down. It's very annoying, to put it mildly.

A week from today our youth society has its first social. We're having a picnic out at a Finca about 25 miles out of the city. (A Finca is a place out in the country that caters to such a type of party; they have recreation facilities, swimming pools, etc.).

Reckon that's about all the news this week. I did receive a letter from pastor Pankow, a former Pastor in Havana and now the editor of a Spanish church magazine. He wants me to write an article on "A Typical Week of a Vicar in Havana" for the magazine, Noticiario de La Fe (News of the Faith). He also wants a few pictures to add to the story. I will have to get busy on that matter soon. He'll have to translate it into Spanish, though, since my Spanish isn't nearly that good.

We had beautiful weather all last week. An average temperature of about 78° F. We had our first rain in about two weeks just a few minutes ago. Wasn't much to speak of, though.

Dave

La Habana, Cuba
November 25, 1957

Dear Dad and Ma,

Don't bother to send any more Christmas cards. I received the ones you sent last week today. If they cost that much to send, it's not worth it. I just may have some of my own made here in Havana. It's pending now. One of my friends has a hobby of making Christmas cards with your pictures on them. She only charges $.10 a piece for them. I was over to one of the members the other day. They had 65 of them that this woman made for them. They're really nice. Since you can't get decent cards here I may as well have some made. In addition to your picture, there is Spanish writing on them plus Mary and the Baby Jesus lying in a manger.

I will be eating my Thanksgiving dinner this Thursday night at one of the American member's homes, the Herr's. I stayed three weeks at their place when I first came down. They're planning to have more of the American families over, so it shouldn't be too lonely.

A week from this Thursday night I'm invited to a cocktail party in honor of Mr. Peterson, one of our American men working at the American Embassy who is leaving Havana to re-join his family in Fort Worth, Texas. If you remember, I stayed at their place when I first came to Cuba. He's a very nice, quiet fellow.

This coming weekend I'll be taking a trip to the Isle of Pines. I plan to go down and visit the vicar who's serving there. On Monday morning, we plan to go deep sea fishing. I surely hope we don't come back empty-handed. I leave Saturday afternoon and will very likely return Monday afternoon.

I took the Renault in to be repaired this morning. Although the cost was not very high, they certainly did a lousy job. I think I could have done as well myself. Pastor said he intends to bring the car down sometime this week and express his displeasure with their work. If that's all the better mechanics they have, they should perhaps close shop.

Yesterday we had a nice attendance in English service again. Another new American family was in attendance; a young couple. She is Missouri Synod Lutheran but he is a Mason, in name only. We also had a Dr. and Mrs.

Berns from St. Louis present. They're here on their honeymoon. Too bad they're not staying because they seem like tremendous people. He's a navy doctor.

Our Spanish service has also been picking up in attendance. The past four Sundays we've had an average of about twenty. That's a large improvement from the average of about five to ten the first months I was down here.

By the way, even with our small mission in Havana, our offerings for the year of 1957 will not be bad at all. While we have a communicant list of about 80, I don't believe more than half of them are actually communicants. I've been checking with some of the families who are on the membership list. It seems they were placed on the list by previous pastors who had never even asked them if they desired to be members. It is this mess that I am supposed to completely clear up before I leave, finding out who really is a communicant and who isn't. Getting back to our offerings. This year they should total $3,000 or a little more. Not bad at all, I don't think. Our average per Sunday is about $70.00.

In place of sending anything for Christmas, I would just as soon have a subscription to *Concordia Theological Monthly*, *Lutheran Witness* and the *Lutheran Layman*. These would be a very satisfactory gift for me. I need some refreshing materials and these periodicals I would especially like. However, if you get me these as a Christmas gift, subscribe to them as soon as possible and send them to my address at the church which is:

Vicar David Dissen
Ave. 27, No. 2611
entre 26 y 30 Calle
La Sierra, Almendares
La Habana, Cuba

It perhaps wouldn't be a bad idea to keep this address handy, for when the Gruell's move from their present apartment into their new house (when ????), you can send my mail (including your letters) to this address.

Talked with Pastor yesterday about how long I would be here. He said to plan until the end of August for he thought he was going to encourage a two-weeks paid vacation for me and therefore I could plan to leave about the middle of August or shortly thereafter. Am letting you know so you can make your vacation plans accordingly. If possible, and you're agreeable, I wouldn't mind going out West, hitting North Dakota and Idaho on the way. It would be nice to visit the churches that Dad has previously served. Just something to let you think about, and also a tentative date as to about when I'll be home.

Dave

5

DECEMBER 1957

Isla de Piños, Cuba
December 3, 1957

Dear Dad and Ma, and Eunice,

Just a few quick lines while I'm still on the Isle of Piños so you can say that you heard from me also while I was on the Isle of Pines. I have only a few minutes yet before my plane leaves for Havana so I'll write as much as I can.

I arrived here in Nueva Gerona, Isla de Piños, about 5:00 p.m. last Saturday afternoon. The airport is quite different than in a large city. Instead of a paved airport it is gravel. The terminal is also very small.

Nueva Gerona is a small town of about 5,000 people. It reminds you very much of a small town in North Dakota or Idaho. The roads are all gravel, and the remainder aren't even that good. They are dirt and old cow trails. Our church here is located on the banks of the Rio de Las Casas (River of the Houses). It is a very small church as the pictures I have of it will show. Also not constructed of the best materials but it is very suitable for its purposes. They plan to build a new church here in the short future.

Sunday afternoon we went out sightseeing. Visited the rock quarry where the prisoners from the main island of Cuba work. Also visited the national reformatory. We couldn't make a total tour of the prison since they didn't have enough guards on duty to take us through. I did buy an ash tray and a pair of book ends (both marble) which were made by the prisoners. They have other very fine hand work for sale at the prison. Most of it was too expensive for the present but if I come down here again, I hope to pick some more up.

Must close from the Isle of Pines now. I will finish the remainder of this letter from the metropolis of Havana, Cuba. Adios for the time being.

I'm back in Havana now, so will try and add a few more lines. I have an adult class in half an hour so won't get too much more out of the way. On Monday morning, we rose bright and early to go out deep sea fishing. The wind was too strong to fish out in the open so we had to settle for a sheltered spot. We went out about 10 miles in the Caribbean Sea on a skiff and then fished in a sheltered stream. No big fish. Only smaller ones. There were four in our party and together we landed about 35 fish. I caught only 2 and my classmate about 5. Instead of using a rod and reel we fished by hand line. There's quite a knack to fishing this way. As a result, I lost most of mine. I had plenty of bites but just didn't catch on fast enough.

We headed back for shore about 10:00 in the morning because my classmate had to be back in Nueva Gerona by 1:00 to catch the plane for the south coast so he could preach down there Monday afternoon. Coming back in, the whitecaps were much higher and we got soaked to the bone. We had to bail water out of the boat with some cans. The fishing was really a lot of fun, though. Then, when we got back to Gerona, we found out that the pilot was sick and would not be able to take us down to the south coast for services. We could have spent all morning and afternoon fishing had we known that.

Monday afternoon we therefore borrowed one of the member's skiffs and went for a cruise up the Rio de Las Cosas. Was a rather long and very beautiful ride. Wish I had my camera along but didn't have it. I had left it in the Pastor's house. Towards the end of the river, we had to pull the motor up and use the oars. Too many stones and other objects were in the way, as well as the water being too shallow for a motor. It is a very fabulous ride. If I get to go up there again, I'll sure take that cruise up the river, with my camera ready.

This morning we went mountain climbing on one of the nearby mountains. Since my classmate's car had broken down yesterday, we hiked it on foot during the morning (about 10 miles in all). Halfway up the mountain we found a cave and went in to explore. Spent about an hour and half in it and examined very nook and cranny possible. Stirred up a nest of bats. We then proceeded to retrace our steps. I thought going down would be much worse than going up, but the opposite was the case. We could slide down the marble boulders and grassy spots on the seat of our pants. We held onto brush and tree branches to break our speed and were down in no time.

This afternoon, before going back to Havana, we headed out to the black sand shores and beaches of Bibijagua. Since the North winds were still acting up, the water was very dirty and full of crud. We did pull down a few coconuts and drink the juice out of them. Later we drove around in the back woods of the Isla de Piños. Very pretty country. Stopped at Jucaro (a fisherman's camp) for a few seconds. Here we met the owner of the place. Turned out he was from Chicago and knew our area in Wisconsin very well. He said he is a very close friend of the owner of Johnson's Wax corporation, with headquarters in Racine. As a matter of fact, at present he's building a summer mansion for the owner of Johnson's Wax right next to his property on the Jucaro River. I mentioned that Eunice had tried to get work there several years ago in their chem lab. He told me just to mention his name to Mr. Johnson and Eunice or anyone would get a job. The name is Vic Barothy. Perhaps Mart could use his name this coming summer if he were interested in chem work. Mr. Barothy said there was a good possibility that Johnson's may open up an experimental lab on the Isle of Pines, since most of the products contained in wax are from Palm trees.

I will continue this after adult class. May I now say that I failed to find Robert Louis Stevenson's treasure on this island. After all, it was the Isle of Pines to which he was referring when he wrote his book, "Treasure Island."

I had a tremendous Thanksgiving dinner last Thursday night. We had Turkey with all the trimmings American style, and also pumpkin pie.

Last Friday was a day that Fidel Castro was supposed to set fire to many ripe sugar cane fields. As a result, Batista's soldiers were on the alert. On my way out to Hershey and on the way back, I was stopped four times for inspection. They search both the car and me. It was the most I've ever been stopped in a period of six hours. I didn't mind the frisking too much but when two of the soldiers were pointing loaded rifles at the back of my head while the third frisked me, well, I just didn't go too much for that. Yet these inspections are very necessary if Cuba is to save their sugar cane crop.

I'm afraid I picked up a poisonous rash while mountain climbing and crawling through the brush on the Isle of Pines. I hope it doesn't take too long to heal. I noticed that my one finger is getting all red and blistered.

Dave

Dear Dad and Ma, (and Professor Dissen),

Temperatures have dropped in Havana since Sunday afternoon so living is more comfortable right now. The high yesterday must have been in the low 70's and doubt if the high today will rise much more. In other words, you know it's about right for me.

Last Wednesday was Santa Barbara Day in Cuba. Santa Barbara is the Patron Saint of the Colored people. While the day is not observed by most of the Cubans, it is very rigidly observed by the African people living in Cuba who belong to the African Voodoo Cult. They are a very superstitious people. They believe that on Santa Barbara Day the gods demand the blood sacrifice of a white haired (blond, naturally) child. Keeping true to form, last Wednesday a blonde child disappeared from one of the hospitals in Havana. This has happened ever since the African Voodoo Cult came to Cuba. Since Pastor Gruell's children are all blondes, they keep a close watch on them come Santa Barbara Day. The Gruell's were warned by the Cubans when they came down here to watch their children on Santa Barbara Day. You never know whose child is going to be kidnapped and sacrificed. They just snatch one and that's it.

Yesterday was Lutheran Church of Cuba conference. Since Pastor Gruell was sick, we had our meeting over in his apartment. Last week all his children were down with the stomach flu and he evidently is finally succumbing to the bug.

Sunday afternoon, I went out to the airport to pick up the vicar from the Isle of Pines who was coming in for our conference yesterday. I lost all my papers plus a rather sizeable amount of cash to a pick-pocket. Yes, I had my back pocket picked as slick as could be. I didn't even know it was missing until later. I could have lost lots more than I did, though, since on Saturday I had cashed my Mission Board check for $240.00. Now I must write in and get a new driver's license, a draft card and social security card. What I intend to do is have Madison, Wisconsin send the necessary information to me. If anything needs to be filled out, I'll fill it out here. Then, I will send it to you and you can enclose the proper amount of money via check to them, asking them to then send the license to me. My reason for this is simple. I would sooner have you send the check because I don't trust the Cuban post office at all, not even when it comes to a check. Therefore, you can send the proper amount to Madison by check after I receive the necessary papers, fill them out and send them to you. I hope you follow this seemingly complicated procedure.

As it stands now, I'm in Cuba without a tourist card or an identification card. This could put me in trouble with the government if I get stopped by the police or Secret Service for an inspection and I have no proper ID papers. All I can tell them is that my wallet was pick-pocketed and they'll have to take that for my answer.

By the way, Eunice, you can give Ma and Dad $20.00 from me and then have Ma transfer it from my account to your account. This again saves me from taking the risk of sending anything through the mails that is in check or cash. I had planned on giving $50.00 but since I lost $60.00 in my wallet someone else can now have a better Christmas. Maybe they need it worse, I don't know.

Dave

Dear Dad and Ma,

I don't know what's happening to me, but I'm going to get this letter off early for a change. I suppose it'll end up getting to you later than ever, though.

As I am writing this letter, a group of Cuban children are going around singing what they classify as Christmas carols. I couldn't quite go along with that. They are singing the Cuban version of "Jingle Bells" plus another song entitled "Navidad" which means "Christmas". There certainly can't be much meaning behind the song for about all it is, is a repetition of Navidad, Navidad, Navidad.

Last night Pastor and I made a call on the United Lutheran couple which is attending our services. A young American couple. He is a member of the United Lutheran Church because he's a Mason. She was brought up Missouri Synod but changed for him. She's still 100% Missouri Synod in belief but she figures only through patient working will she eventually have her prayers answered and that her husband will ask for a demit from the lodge. We had quite a good talk with him on the lodge last night and the door is practically open for me to now start instructions with him. I surely hope he goes through with it. He hasn't missed a Sunday since they've been here and she figures as long as he is going with HER to HER church, it's best to be patient.

Thanks to this families' generosity, I now have a radio in my room. They had a Zenith radio which had the dial knob on it broken. He said they haven't used it in years and I was more than welcome to use it. There's a little trick to dialing it but it can be done. Thus, this morning I had music during breakfast for the first time in months. This afternoon I heard Lawrence Tibbett, the baritone, sing part of the opera of THE MASKED BALL. If you remember, I have that on the other side of my Figaro record. It was really good to hear something familiar again.

Evidently this past week just wasn't meant for me. Not only did I lose my wallet and about $60.00 cash to a pick-pocket; I also lost a $10.00

pair of wash and dry dress pants (the best pair I had). Someone stole them off the clothesline of the people who do my wash. I don't mind making contributions to the poor and needy. I only wish that they would change their methods of asking (actually, they really didn't ask in the first place). What I should say, is that I hope they revise their tactics of receiving.

Tuesday afternoon I went to the police station to report my loss by thievery. Finally, after being shifted around from one precinct to the other, I ended up at the Tourist Police. They were anything but cooperative. They were too concerned about their game of checkers to help anyone. They took my name and address and went back to their game.

I had quite an experience the other night. One of the young American couples I'm instructing made a rather startling revelation. She was ALC but now is taking our instruction. To show you how thoroughly the ALC instruct their people, after the lesson (which was on Law and Gospel) she told me that she didn't know there was a difference between Law and Gospel. She had never been taught it. She was really glad to be made aware of the difference and also aware of the importance of making the distinction.

By the way, my $60.00 loss to an unknown pick-pocket received an unexpected shock absorber on Wednesday of this week. I received a $50.00 Christmas check from the Mission Board of Latin and South American. All which goes to show that the Lord takes care of things in his own way.

Good Shepherd congregation in Mexico City, Mexico (which was my original Vicarage assignment before being changed to Havana, Cuba) will be receiving their vicar after all. Yesterday Pastor Gruell received word from the Mission Board that Pastor Otto Zeeb felt that he had to hand in his resignation because of his wife's health. Since Pastor Gruell is head of the foreign missions in Cuba, he was instructed to inform the vicar on the Isle of Pines that he would be going to Mexico City in February and finish out his vicarage there. You see, the vicar on the Isle of Pines is there only during the furlough of the resident pastor. The resident pastor returns the end of January so that frees them from the need of a vicar. We had hoped to have the vicar come over to Havana and work in the Spanish field. That's definitely out now. Guess I will not have a roommate or the company that I had looked forward to.

I would appreciate very much receiving a set of U.S. Income Tax blanks as soon as possible. I do not intend to pay any tax on my vicarage salary. I wrote to the Sem and they sent me the necessary information to guide me in filing my report. I can claim exemption of my salary on the basis that it is a scholarship grant, preparing me for further study in my 4th year. Naturally, the Supreme Court hasn't passed a definite ruling on this exception yet. So far, no test case has been made of it. Eventually it may come to that.

I wrote the Mission Board and asked them to increase the amount of money sent home to you to $50.00 or $60.00 per month. I don't remember exactly now which it was but you'll know when they send it. Then you can let me know.

I'll be preaching Christmas morning at Hershey; 8:00 services. That means early rising as I'll have to leave about 6:00 a.m.

Walt's bowling is simply unbelievable. Maybe beginner's luck. Dad's should be improving for he's much better than a 145 man.

Dave

P.S. Please save the pictures I enclose.

La Habana, Cuba
December 23, 1957

Dear Dad and Ma,

Last night was our Christmas program. We really had a nice turn out. With the children present, we had well over 100 in attendance. I didn't get to see too much of the program. I had to run around and pick up several children that failed to show up. Thus, the program was about half finished when I returned.

To make matters worse, Pastor Gruell's smallest girl (1½) was sick with a fever and a cold. Since Mrs. Gruell was the organist, they bundled Mary up and took her along. They left Mary in the lounge with one of the members but she didn't do too well with her. She started kicking up a fuss so I had to go back and take care of her. It ended up that I played nursemaid for about an hour and a half. They finally relieved me of her about 9:30, just in time for me to take the bus load of children back home (another 2-hour stint). Thus, you can see that I wasn't really able to enjoy the Christmas program.

Saturday evening Pastor and I took in the Christmas program at our parochial day school out in Reparto Marti. Man, you can really see the advantage in putting on a program when the children can practice every day. Their program really went off slick. They had the right children for the right parts. They acted like professional actors and actresses. Their singing was also very good.

Outside Christmas trees and decorations are very conspicuously absent in Cuba this year. Why? It's because Fidel Castro has sent out personal letters to many citizens warning them that whoever has a Christmas tree in their house will receive a present from Santa Claus (not through the chimney but through their window) in the form of a bomb. The people are scared stiff, believe me. Also, Castro sent letters to many people warning them not to celebrate Christmas Eve and New Year's Eve. He said there would be plenty of trouble if they did. Everyone is looking for a possible revolution by the first of the year.

Tomorrow (Christmas Eve), the pagan people in Cuba kill the fatted pig and observe one of their biggest wining and dining feasts of the year. Roast pork rum, and cognac will be flowing free and easy. It is thus that these pagan and superstitious people celebrate what should be the most joyous eve of all people.

I really had a wonderful experience talking with the one Cuban girl that I'm instructing after the program last night. She told me that she had been crying all through the program. She said the wonderful story of her Savior filled an emptiness that had long existed in her heart. She said she had never seen anything like it in the Catholic or Pentecostal Church. She has been attending our services for the past four Sundays and began taking instructions last Thursday.

It really does one good to hear another tell you how happy and contented they are to have found salvation in their Savior. As she said, she had seen so much sin and corruption in Havana that she doubted if she ever would find a true church. She said that she has found that now and really lets it show in her life and her activity in the church, even though she isn't a member. She'll be a good solid Christian when she is confirmed.

This Wednesday I'll be going out to Hershey for Christmas morning services at 8:30. That means rising very early. I didn't get a chance to write my Christmas Day sermon until today. I have tomorrow yet in which to study it. Last Friday, I was stopped six times for inspection by the soldiers on my way to Hershey. A couple of them tried to give me trouble so I just pretended I didn't understand what they were saying in Spanish. After a couple of minutes of frustration on their part, they would look at one another, say: "Americano" and motion me to "dale" (go ahead). If you don't want to waste time with the soldiers, just act stupid (no acting necessary on my part) and they'll let you pass.

Tomorrow evening I'll be spending with the Gruell's. Pastor told me if we were going to keep custom with the pagans, we might as well do it in the minister's house. We will open our presents then. I have to buy for their children tomorrow, yet.

By the way, you trusted the Cuban mail and won out. I'll never know how that happened but by the grace of God. You know, all constitutional guarantees are still revoked (and probably will be until next June). That means we have no guarantee of protection whatsoever, including the mails. The past week I've had several letters and Christmas cards come to me that have been opened and checked for censorship. Man, don't take any more foolish chances. You're just asking for trouble.

Well, "Aguinaldo" time is just about past. What is an "Aguinaldo?" An Aguinaldo is an unspontaneous Christmas gift that you are obligated to pay to everyone that serves you, such as water man, mail man, garbage collector, paper boy, maid, etc. During Christmas, Havana is truly the city of "palms." These people ring your doorbells and just stand waiting. You've got to give them something or it's too bad. And they don't miss.

I would appreciate very much if you would send me income tax blanks for this year. Send me both the long and short forms as I am yet undecided which I'll use. Deduct the cost from my bank account for mailing costs.

So much for now. May you all have a Christ-filled Christmas.

Dave

Home where services were held in Central Hershey.

La Habana, Cuba
December 28, 1957

Dear Dad, Ma, and Eunice,

Well, Christmas, 1957 is history and there was no snow included in it for me. On Christmas Day, the temperatures were in the low 80's so you can see there wasn't too much a possibility for any of that white stuff. I sort of got a charge out of Fred's letter. On the flap of the envelope, he writes "Have a white Christmas, sonny!"

This afternoon I received my first package from the U.S. since arriving here. It was two wiffle balls from cousin Ernie Baese's family in St. Louis. I don't know how in the world they ever cleared customs without me having to pay duty. They came through, though. Pastor Gruell was also amazed that they came in duty free.

On Christmas morning, I had services at Hershey, 8:30 a.m. I had to get up at 4:30 a.m. Christmas morning, which was quite early. Especially when you take into consideration that I was up until midnight Christmas Eve with the Gruell's. There was a turnout of 14 for Christmas Day services there, which is several above-average. Also, for the first time the husband of one of the members came to our services. He was also there last night for services so maybe he'll be a regular attender now.

Christmas Eve we had the regular Cuban Christmas food. Mrs. Gruell fixed up a lot of pork chops with all the trimmings. Pork is the Cuban meal on Christmas eve. Afterwards we had a short devotion, singing of carols and then opening of the gifts. The children really liked the toys I had bought them. Their little girl played with the pull toy I bought her all night. And naturally, Pop Gruell and the boys stayed up until 1:00 Christmas morning playing with the dart gun and funny face target I had bought for the smallest boy. We really had a tremendous time. I received a beautiful sports shirt from the Gruell's. I am wearing it for the first time today.

Christmas Day evening was spent over at the Hedin's for a turkey supper. Afterwards, their next-door neighbors dropped in so we had an evening of conversation in Spanish. He is an old retired mail carrier and she is one of these understanding elderly women who was more than willing to help me with my Spanish. She took things very slow and as a result I understood practically everything. I was able to take part in the conversation and picked up quite a few new words for my Spanish vocabulary. That's the kind of thing I need more often to help my Spanish.

Pastor went down to Boca de Galafre this past Thursday for Christmas Day services there. It was rather gloomy, believe me. No celebrations whatsoever. Some people who dared to put up trees found it very costly. Their houses were burned to the ground. Fidel Castro has those people in the southern part of the island scared of their own shadows. There just wasn't any outward sign of Christmas joy present at all. That's something most of the people in the States take for granted.

By the way, you can thank all the members that sent me cards. I was, to put it mildly, very surprised to receive as many cards as I did from the members in Union Grove. Also, I will be awaiting my income tax (both forms) blanks in the near future.

Just an added thought. Since there was no news from Ma last week because she was sick, there should be twice as much in her next letter. Hope she is feeling better soon and won't have to wait to add a triple amount the next time she writes.

Dave

Cuban congregation in Havana.
Pastor and Mrs. Gruell pictured at the extreme right.

6

JANUARY 1958

Dear Dad and Ma,

If I stay one up all the time, I'll never get behind. That's why I'm getting this letter off early this week.

I really had an enjoyable New Year's Day this year. In the morning, I went to Spanish service. In the afternoon Pastor, one of our American members, and I went out on the links for several hours. It was only my second game of golf but I did enjoy it tremendously. I lost only one ball and got off a few tremendous drives. As a matter of fact, they both told me that for my second game I did very well. I shot a 67. Tomorrow afternoon I hope to go out again with Pastor and this same member.

New Year's Day evening Pastor, his wife, and I were invited over to this American families' house for supper. We enjoyed some real good American food, believe me. In the evening, we had one of the best religious discussions I've been present at. A Cuban friend of this family, who is Catholic (only by name), happened to drop in and the discussion was on. It began about 8:00 and we finally rounded it up at 1:00 A.M. January 2, 1958. Man, I'm telling you, Pastor Gruell is a very solid LCMS pastor from my observations. It was a F A B U L O U S discussion.

New Year's Eve we had English services and communion. It was very poorly attended but that was expected since Havana has so much to offer the people at all times. One enlightening aspect, though, was the presence of about seven visitors. A couple were Lutherans and the others were Methodists etc. who happened to see our notice of services in the paper.

Last night the 8th Northern Wind of the season started kicking up a fuss. It's the worst we have had so far. Overnight, a small tidal wave came in next to the Gruell's apartment. It really did a lot of damage. It flooded all the basements in the vicinity and blocked all the roads running parallel to the ocean for a good three blocks. They couldn't park the car next to their apartment at all. Wood, boulders, driftwood, sand and everything imaginable was washed up on the streets. They had to evacuate several nearby families overnight. Man, I can see now why water can be so destructive. You see the mess it leaves behind and you never forget it. The way the waves are kicking up again tonight, I wouldn't be surprised if another wave came in. The water is splashing spectacularly – over 100 feet high in places.

Talking about the winds, we have had yesterday and today, they also left their effect on the palm and other trees, uprooting many and blocking much traffic. The wind also left its mark on my bathroom above our church worship facility. It sucked a big window right out, frame and all, smashing it on the ground below. Since torrential rains accompanied the wind, I now have a bathroom filled with water.

New Year's Eve the people really celebrated here. I stayed up and watched the New Year in over at Pastor's. At midnight, the police shot off machine guns, canons, pistols and every other type of arms they had. Surprisingly, I heard only three bombs go off all night. One was when I was at the Spanish service out at Reparto Marti (10-11:00 at night)! It was very close. You could feel the building vibrate.

This Sunday our new church service schedule goes into effect. We will now have English service at 9:00 and Spanish at 11:00. This is because we are working for an indigenous church in Havana and feel that the Spanish service should be the late service.

By the way, last Saturday night, I watched the first double header I've seen in about a month and a half. My team came through in fine fashion, winning 1-0. Dick Brodowsky gained his 12th decision in that victory. He has pitched magnificent ball in this Cuban Winter League. Whoever has him has an up-and-coming young pitcher. I believe he belongs to Philadelphia but I may be mistaken.

Talking about baseball, the Cuban Winter League sent five U.S. major league players back to the States. They accused them of goofing off while they were down here and wanted nothing more to do with them. You probably read about it in the newspapers.

I sure was glad to see the Rose Bowl game and other bowl games turn out the way they did. This was the year I should have entered the Bowl Contest selections. New Year's Day at dinner, Pastor ran down the list of all bowl games, asking me who I was picking (he's a tremendous sports fan). Without having seen the paper and knowing who was favored, I gave him my answers. Lo and behold, the next day Pastor informed me that I had picked every winner, without one wrong. How's that for luck!

I am catching up on a little bit of U.S. popular music right now. I suppose I'll be way behind on that when I return. I have very little time to listen to it and when I do, I don't always find a station that carries it.

Had a New Year's card and short note from Elsie Braun today. It was good hearing from her.

Dave

P.S. Now that I've let you think about my 67 golf score, I'll confess that it was only for 9 holes. Tremendous, right?

Also, a reminder for both types of income tax blanks with instructions.

Only wrote five letters tonight, so right now my head is swimming.

La Habana, Cuba
January 10, 1958

Dear Dad and Ma,

I received the income tax blanks and information today. Thanks. Now I'll be able to take care of Uncle Sam. What a pleasant thought. I also received my first issues of the *Lutheran Witness*, only that was last week. I guess they started my subscription with the first of December. Only things I miss in the Witness are the supplements.

I haven't as yet heard anything on my driver's license. If I don't hear by tomorrow, I'll write again. I've never seen any-one so slow in answering. I did finally receive a duplicate of my draft card. However, they failed to list my classification on it.

Too bad you've been having so much snow up there. For some odd reason, I can't say that I've particularly missed the snow as yet. We've had some rather cold weather ourselves. Temperatures have been down in the high 50's and middle 60's. That makes it very cold here since they have no heating facilities whatsoever. At least I've been able to wear my woolen suit and a few of my flannel shirts a couple times this past week. I didn't think I'd ever get them out of mothballs.

I learned from Pastor Gruell this past week that I've now joined the elite class that he belongs to. He informed me that the German speaking colony of our congregation is now using me as a topic of discussion in their bull sessions. They claim that I don't give them any rest in my efforts to get them to attend church. One member told Pastor that I should let up on them a little, that Germans like to go their own way and at their own convenience. That won't discourage me. I'll just give them more to talk about. This week alone I've made at least 10 German calls. The thing is, they have nothing to complain about because they don't even as much as dent the church door. Only about two German families are regular church goers. The rest you seldom, if ever, see. What they like is a religion that lets them alone.

Tomorrow begins the grind of Saturday School and frayed nerves again. The two-week vacation was a welcome one, believe me. However, you cannot begin to minimize the importance of this school. It's doing wonders

68

for these children. I'm definitely sold on Saturday school, there's no getting around it.

I suppose Mrs. Wischow did hold things down somewhat. Yet, knowing that when Fred, Mart and Walt get together with Dad, I'll bet she didn't put too much of a cramp into things. Walt said that they just had to give her something to keep the fireside chats in Beach going strong.

I don't know for sure where the Steve Allen TV show is being televised from. It is very likely one of the night club spots. If at all possible, I will try and make it, that is, if it's financially possible. Just look for someone drinking a toast and it'll be me.

I will admit that Ma did get off to a good start in the New Year but what happened to Dad? Not even as much as a pen scratch on the last letter. Though Uncle Vic may be sick, he can still at least sign an X.

I was glad to hear that you received those last pictures. I was just beginning to wonder if they were going through the mail or not because I hadn't heard anything on any of the other pictures I sent. I thought perhaps they were censoring them.

Dave

P.S. I have played four games of golf in all and in the 4th game I broke the high 50's for nine holes. I shot a 59. They tell me that's mighty good for someone who's played only four rounds of the sport. It's a tremendous game. I have my most trouble with the wood irons. When I use the plain irons, I'm okay. On my tee shots, I've had several 200 plus yard drives, not bad huh?

Sunday night was the eve of celebration for the Cuban Christmas, preparatory to the Tres Reyes (Three Kings) on Monday (our Epiphany). Stores were open all day Sunday and special booths were set up in the streets with bargains galore. About 11:00 Sunday night, Pastor and I went down to look for used bikes for his children. Just to see the milling thousands of people on the streets and sidewalks is an experience. It's simply amazing, the way they go all out here. The Tres Reyes is the day that the Cubans give away their presents.

By the way, I hope to begin instructing a Chinese family in the near future, God-willing. He happened to attend our church by accident and I've talked to him several times since. He's definitely interested. He attended a Christian school in China over ten years ago but since has been away from the church. He works in the Chinese Bank here in Havana.

Dave

La Habana, Cuba
January 21, 1958

Dear Dad and Ma,

At least if there's no mail heading this way from Wisconsin, I'll try and keep the pony express moving from this end, even if it's a mite later than usual this week.

Have been kept very busy until now. Vicar Sudbrock, from the Isle of Pines, came in Sunday afternoon. This is his last trip up to Havana before his departure for Mexico. We have vowed to make it a memorable one by showing him as much of Cuba as possible.

Yesterday (Monday), was spent on a picnic with him all day. We visited the Hershey sugar refinery and Jibacca (the J is pronounced like an h). We ate our picnic lunch at Hershey Gardens, one of the most beautiful picnic grounds I've ever seen. If the pictures I took turned out good, I'll send a few of them.

Today I was up bright and early and we headed out to Veradero, a world-famous summer resort on the northern coast of Cuba. A trip of about 90 miles. We had a lousy day of rain so didn't get any good pictures. We returned about 6:00 tonight. Spent only about 2 hours at the place. We saw as much as we could with the unpleasant weather conditions hampering us.

Also, with us these past two days on our excursions was a Missouri Synod Lutheran American couple who were visiting Havana. A couple by the name of Mr. and Mrs. Marchmann who are from Cincinnati. Very wonderful people. They leave tomorrow for the States. Some of the finest Christian people I've met. One's faith was very much edified by talking and being with them.

Had a letter from the "110" Mission Club at the Sem, the group which is paying the salaries of us four foreign vicars. On February 6th, 1958, they're having a special "110 Day" emphasis at the Seminary, in which both morning and evening chapels will be dedicated to prayer and services for us four. They asked me to get in contact with a ham radio operator, send his call signal to St. Louis, and then prepare and deliver a ten-minute talk on my work in Cuba over live radio broadcast through this ham operator. They want to hear from all four of us directly in our fields of work. We are supposed to be hooked up for the night chapel service (10:00 p.m.). They will tell us what time to cut in. If I can't get hold of a ham operator, then I'm supposed to make a 10-minute tape recording and send it to them by the 6th. That means getting on the ball right pronto. It could be that Uncle Charlie and a few other relatives would be able to hear me if they were present that night.

I take it Dad must have become lost in the snowstorms that hit Wisconsin. Not hearing from him two weeks in a row means something drastic must have happened.

I bought a 35 mm. camera last week. I took my first pictures with it yesterday and today. Hope they turn out good. Took only black and white pictures because of my unfamiliarity with the new-fangled thing. I hope to go to colored slides soon.

Last night, I went to a show with Pastor Gruell and wife, Vicar Sudbrock and the Marchmanns. Afterwards, we took them to their place of lodging at the Hotel Nacional. We had a short night cap (one beer) and were fortunate enough to see (free of charge, by peeking through the curtain) their star singing attraction in their night show, Anna Maria Alberghetti. She's a fabulous singer! World renowned.

God-willing, I will embark on the initial answer to my prayer of being able to instruct this Chinese man I previously talked about this Wednesday night (tomorrow). Last week I paid him a visit. It was one of my most gratifying and blessed experiences since being here. This experience in itself will be worth my entire year in Cuba. You just can't beat working with these contacts who come from heathen countries and by God's grace come under your shepherding. The joy of telling one such person about his Savior and having him accept Jesus in humble faith through the power of the Holy Spirit is inexpressible in words. You can only feebly explain what it does to you.

So much for now. I trust that I'll hear this week from Wisconsin. Maybe you need to hire someone to shovel the sidewalks so you can get out and mail your letters.

Dave

Dear Dad and Ma,

I have spent a futile day so far with Missionary Glienke, so I may as well take time off to write a few lines also. He and his family arrived Saturday night from their six months furlough in the States on their way to the Isle of Pines. Today he was supposed to clear his car through customs so they could leave tomorrow for the Isle of Pines. As it was, everything was fouled up and he didn't get to first base today. That means another rat race with him tomorrow.

Saturday afternoon I made contact with the radio ham operator who is to broadcast my ten-minute report to the Sem. While I was at his house, he picked up a ham in Knoxville, Tenn. and told him he had a young American who would like to say a few words. We ended up talking back and forth for about half an hour. The ham in Knoxville was really thrilled because it was his first contact with a foreign ham operator. This is really fascinating work, this ham radio operator. It doesn't cost you a cent and you can talk anywhere in the world as long you have made connections with another ham. Perhaps you could find a ham operator in your vicinity and we could talk back and forth for a-while some time. You'd have to get his name, address and call numbers. Then send them to me and this fella, who is willing to make any contacts for me, will be able to pick him up.

This morning the Secret Police thoroughly searched the apartment of one of our church members. Exactly why, they did not say. The poor woman was a bundle of nerves by the time they finished. They didn't miss ripping up a thing in their search. Now I can see why so many of the Cubans feel insecure. The police just march in unannounced and take over.

We really had a swell attendance in English services yesterday. An even 40 were present. That is very good, for since the first of the year when English services were switched to 9:00 from the previous 11:00, attendance has been bad. Maybe the Americans are finally getting accustomed to the earlier hour.

I received my first parking ticket the other day. It was at one of those places where you are supposed to know by foreknowledge that parking isn't permitted. There were no signs posted anywhere about "No Parking," but a nice little green piece of paper was hanging on the windshield when I came out. It only costs a buck. The secretary of our church will go to court and take care of it. She has to go for Pastor's wife also. She also received a ticket several days earlier.

I never did receive your letter of two weeks ago. I suppose it was because it was never written.

CPH certainly is lousy when it comes to sending the *Lutheran Witnesses*. They wait until about four or five pile up on you and then send them all at once. They are paid to send it out issue by issue, not monthly or when-ever they feel like it.

I have my LLL Membership Card but still no Lutheran Layman Paper as of this time. I have no idea why they are so slow in arriving here. Perhaps the postal department. I'm beginning to wonder if perhaps they're just as bad as the Publishing House.

So much for now. We have had the most humid weather in Havana last week that they've had in many years. It caused the plaster to fall off many ceilings and walls. We lost a big hunk of plaster in church.

Dave

7

FEBRUARY 1958

La Habana, Cuba
February 3, 1958

Dear Dad and Ma, and Eunice,

I have a few minutes yet before my 9:00 adult instruction class tonight, so will get the show on the road at any rate. I will finish when I get back if I have the time.

The mystery of your letter dated January 12 was resolved this past week. However, another mystery developed upon receipt of it. The postman said it was registered and made me sign for it. To tell the truth, I failed to see why you sent it registered (if you did such a thing?). It doesn't seem like Dad to send an ordinary letter as registered mail. Perhaps you have the answer to this mystery. Or else someone in the post office, somewhere, goofed again.

Another Norther started blowing in again today and has really sent the temperatures tumbling. Boy, it feels good to put on a few woolen clothes again.

Yesterday, Pastor Gruell, his wife and I went out to the Havana Biltmore golf course to watch the close of the Woman's Professional Golf Tournament. I got pictures of Jackie Pung and Faye Crocker. Also, Betsy Rawls. Jackie Pung was leading by four strokes yesterday going into the final nine rounds. Then she blew it royally and lost in a sudden death play-off with Faye Crocker. Man, that Crocker really played some tremendous golf. She took the tournament on the first hole of the sudden death play-off with a 20-foot putt. A real beauty of a shot.

"Hasta lluego hasta once o manana." Well, here it is morning, and I'm just finishing this letter. I woke up a few minutes ago but no thanks to the alarm clock. Several times of late the alarm has failed to go off.

With the congregation in Union Grove as large as it is now, there's no reason why they shouldn't be able to hire a secretary for a couple of days a week. I'm sure there'd be enough to keep one busy. Or better yet, why not have one or several of the members volunteer to do the work. We have one member in our church who is doing that. It really helps a lot.

I still have a few last-minute things to iron out if I intend to be hooked up with St. Louis Thursday evening. They're sort of bogging down on their end. I haven't heard a word from them in two and a half weeks. I have no idea why they have been so silent.

Last week Friday, I was over at the ham radio operators. He contacted a ham in Guatemala who happened to know both our Lutheran missionaries over there, Missionary Schrank and Missionary Bretscher. I had set an appointment yesterday morning to talk with Missionary Schrank but we were unable to contact Guatemala. Conditions were poor.

I finally received the December 31 edition of the *Lutheran Witness* yesterday. A few days later the January 13 one arrived. I still have not received an LLL Paper.

I have both my driver's license and draft card. All I need now is my social security card and I'll be in business again.

As far as telephone calls are concerned, there'll be none from Miami until April 22-25. Those are the approximate dates of our spring conference in Miami.

Dave

La Habana, Cuba
February 9, 1958

Dear Dad, Ma, and Eunice,

I'm sorry to hear that the flu bug laid every one low. We've avoided it so far down here (that is, Pastor Gruell's family and I). However, I've got what you could call my first real cold and sore throat since I've been here. It came on last night and really made it miserable preaching this morning. I'm telling you, with all the quick changes in temperature we've had so far, it's amazing I haven't had more colds. Cuba may be the land of perpetual summer but when you aren't prepared for high 40 and low 50-degree weather, you get mighty uncomfortable. And they aren't prepared for it here.

I received a radio-cablegram from St. Louis this past Wednesday morning. They asked me to make my broadcast Wednesday night instead of Thursday. This is because they wanted to tape-record it for Thursday night.

Well, I finally got through to them about 10:15 at night our time. The ham operator spoke little English so I had to take care of calling St. Louis and make the contact. It's really an experience. After about 10 minutes we had our wave length frequencies adjusted and then we received and were received very clearly. It was just like sitting in the front room and talking to them. They said they heard us very clearly and we copied them the same. All in all, we talked about an hour. It really seemed good to be able to talk to some old Sem friends.

I think that if you'd do some checking, you'd find plenty of ham operators in Racine. I looked in the World Radio Amateur Address Book and saw several people in Racine listed. If you find someone with a good powerful set, arrangements can be made to talk with one another. This fellow that let me use his set Wednesday night has a very strong set. Not only that, he is situated on one of the highest hills in Havana so he is able to pick up practically everything.

I wasn't able to give a true report on current conditions in Cuba today because I knew that I was under censorship and that I had to be careful about what I said. Thus, I wasn't able to report on the actual political situation or its effect on the church.

Now that constitutional guarantees have been restored, things are starting to pop again. Several weeks ago, the rebels seized two radio stations in Havana and forced them to broadcast anti-Batista propaganda for several minutes. Last night, many TV viewers saw armed rebels seize one of the main TV stations for several minutes and make them play anti-Batista recordings. Last Monday night, about 9:00 my ears were buzzed but good by a bomb that went off. I was on my way to adult instruction class and passed within 2 ½ blocks of it when it went off. It was set outside a bank and really messed up the place. The government reported that it was one of the most powerful bombs to explode since the rebels had begun their activities. Tuesday night seven more bombs were set off in Havana but all less powerful. I wouldn't be too surprised to see a revolution in Cuba within a short time. Now that guarantees have been restored, people are moving about more freely and are acting more boldly.

My duplicate driver's license arrived about four weeks ago. I am now set as far as my draft card and driver's license are concerned.

Last Thursday, Vicar Sudbrock arrived from the Isle of Pines to begin serving in Spanish work out at Reparto Marti, a suburb of Havana. He is from Indianapolis. He knows Uncle Walter and Aunt Greta.

I also heard that Bill was to be laid off. I didn't think conditions were that bad. He should have never quit the railroad. I still think that offered him more security than did his other work. Sure, he may have been bounced around for two or three years but then he would have been set. I sure hope he is called back soon. After all, he's got a wife and a family and a house to pay for.

Dave

La Habana, Cuba
February 10, 1958

Dear Dad, Ma, and Eunice,

Cool weather still prevails in what is supposed to be a sunny clime. We've really had our share of it this winter but I won't complain. Guess I picked a good year in which to head South because from reports I've read the United States is really having a dilly of a winter.

Still haven't received any Lutheran Laymen League. If I knew where to write, I'd write and try to find out what the problem is. After all, that subscription should have started at least with the first of the year. If they're that bad in filling their subscriptions, they're even worse than CPH (If that's possible?).

I finally opened a bank account in Havana. I figured it was much safer than keeping my money in the room. Not only that, the money may not disappear as fast either. Unless you watch yourself, it really goes fast. Everything is so high here that you can have a pretty bare cupboard by the end of the month. I'm glad you're now getting $60.00 a month from the Mission Board. That should give me a little something in savings when I return.

I still have my income tax forms to fill out and send in. I've been waiting to hear from Stix, Baer and Fuller but haven't received a thing. I can't do anything until I get their withholding slips. I don't intend to pay any tax on my vicarage earnings. I am told that my salary can be declared as deductible since it's the same as a scholarship. Otherwise, I'd probably have to borrow to pay my tax. This receiving a State-side salary of $185.00 per month but a Cuban salary of $270.00 per month would really hurt when it comes to paying taxes. Actually, you need the $270.00 to live down here and as a result I would have about an extra $100 per month on which to pay taxes. This would soon count up.

This week our Lenten services begin. We have Spanish services at 8:00 Wednesday nights and English at 8:00 Thursday nights. Only yesterday, Pastor Gruell told me that he would do all the Lenten preaching. He said that if I wanted to volunteer for any of the services it would be okay, but he wasn't expecting it. That way it won't cramp me so much in sermon writing.

I suppose Dad read that Cuba won the Caribbean World Series. I see that Casey Wise, according to the Miami Herald Sunday newspaper, is listed as Braves property. If so, the Braves really have a good prospect. He played for the Caribbean Champs, the Marianao Tigers. I saw several games in which he played during the Winter League here in Havana. He really looks sharp.

Nothing at all like the Casey Wise who played for the Cubs last year. His hitting was good. All good solid liners. He hit right at the players many times but they claim that is a good indication of an up-and-coming hitter when he hits line-drives. And believe me, that's just what he was doing all winter long. I wouldn't be surprised to see him take Red Schoendienst's place in a year or two.

Pastor Gruell goes to St. Louis on March 17 to meet with the Mission Board. He is going to get the ball rolling on the building of the church and parsonage in Havana. We hope to have it started by May 1st. Both projects, that is.

Dave

Dear Dad, Ma, and Eunice,

Better get this off tonight yet if I want to get it off at all this week. I have to preach for Lenten Services this Thursday night so my time will be well spent.

Good thing I don't have too many weeks like this past one. One of the American families quit taking their adult instruction classes. Another woman who is on our communicant membership list sent me a long 8-page epistle on her religious beliefs. It's enough to make your hair stand on end. I will very definitely save it for posterity. I must also save it for possible disciplinary purposes. If she really believes what she wrote, the only thing that can be done is to re-confirm what she said and unless a change happens, then drop her from the communicant membership list. These two things in themselves were enough to make the week rather depressing.

I did have a wonderful picker-upper with the Chinese man I'm instructing, though! He's taking a real interest in the Bible. This past week on the review lesson we had he came through with flying colors. Of everyone that's gone through that particular lesson's review, he's done by far the best. With his limited religious background, it speaks well for his interest and his understanding of the Bible. It just goes to show what a person will do when he's really interested in learning the truth from God's Word.

Last week Monday, I went golfing with pastor Gruell, his wife and Vicar Sudbrock. Pastor took me by only five strokes. He shot a 52 and I came in with a 57. This was only my fifth round of golf so I feel pretty good about the 57. If I keep lowering my score by two strokes every time, I'll be satisfied.

This afternoon we were out to watch the trial runs of the warm-ups for the Cuban Grand Prix tomorrow. We had to pay a $1.50 for our tickets (which are also good for tomorrow) but we had dandy spots to watch from. We were right on the point of the curve that the sports cars took about 60-80 miles per hour.

As a result, we got to see three crack-ups. One car and its driver ended up about 10 feet in front of me. I was the only one of the spectators with their camera ready so I got a good picture right after he quit spinning. I hope it turns out good. I also got a shot of another driver just a split second before he wrecked. I just ran out of film about five minutes before the major wreck. This fellow really went out of control, completely putting his car out of commission. He came out unscratched, as did the other drivers. His car hit several bales of hay, did a few turns (spins, that is) and came to rest on top of a few more bales of hay right alongside the track.

If the pictures turn out good, I did get a couple of shots (close-ups) of the major trial runs. One of the fellas standing ahead of me was from the press. He asked me if I'd like to go to the very edge of the curve where spectators were forbidden and get a few shots. I said yes, so he talked to the soldiers and we were given the "go-ahead" sign. I was only about 10 feet from Juan Fangio when he came into the turn doing about 80 per hour. I also got a picture of Stirling Moss when he came into the turn. It's living dangerous but it's fun.

This race is one of the biggest sports car races in the world. It draws all the leading racers, such as Fangio, Moss, Behra, Shelby, Godlia, (even Porfirio Rubirosa) etc.

Tomorrow the races begin at 9:00. The main race is 300 kilometers. This is the one that all your world-famous racers take part in. I plan to be on hand with plenty of film and get a few colored pictures. There should be thrills aplenty.

Tomorrow morning, we have another appointment with the ham radio operator to talk to the missionary in Guatemala. We plan to make this a monthly appointment.

Tuesday Pastor Gruell's wife's parents are coming in for a two weeks visit. He is Professor Bretscher, from the Seminary in St. Louis. He is one of Synod's outstanding men on secret organizations, especially the Masonic Lodge.

I'll bet Ma and Aunt Esther had a good time in Milwaukee. Such a trip is good for Ma. Just what she needs for a change. More of them wouldn't hurt anything at all.

I had a letter from Uncle Charlie informing me about Aunt Clara. Her condition I do not know about either. He did say that the doctor said that he got it all. I have heard nothing at all about Uncle Wally. He'd better take a good rest while he's at it. He needs it.

The mystery of the "registered letter" shall remain a mystery. It has already been destroyed. Believe me, I don't intend to lose any sleep over it.

Talking about sleep, about time I hit the sack. Believe it or not, the weather in Havana is finally warming up. Today was the warmest day we've had in about two months. I suppose now it will get ungodly warm.

Dave

8

MARCH 1958

La Habana, Cuba
March 3, 1958

Dear Dad and Ma, and Eunice,

The II Gran Prix of Cuba was cut rather short last Monday afternoon. On the 6th lap one of Cuba's amateur drivers lost control of his powerful sports car and crashed into a crowd of spectators. Finals as far as the death toll is concerned: seven killed and 31 injured (mostly seriously). The tragedy occurred on the straight-a-way, not too far from where we were.

I did manage to get several pictures before the race was called off at the end of six laps. I snapped two wrecks on the curve on which I was standing (same place as last Sunday afternoon). There's not much doubt that the track was a hazard. The curve on which we were was really slick. That accounts for the two wrecks on that curve in the first six laps.

I do have a newspaper that I want to send you when I get around to it. They have the story and pictures of the fatal accident. One magazine I bought has tremendous pictures of the accident. They have a series of three shots showing the car as it is jumping the curb, as it hits the spectators and bodies are catapulted into the air, and finally when it comes to rest with the driver flung over the hood.

The accident was only a sad climax to the day. Why? It's because the people were very angry about the rebels kidnapping Fangio. Naturally, Fangio was unable to race Monday since he was still held captive by the time the race was to start. They didn't release him until midnight, Monday.

Well, I wish the race would have gone all 90 laps but it is enough to wet my appetite for big sports car racing. It is really a thrill to watch those guys in operation.

Last Tuesday, Pastor Gruell's folks-in-law arrived from St. Louis. They knew Uncle Ed's family well. They said that Aunt Clara died from a blood clot. I understand that she passed away on Tuesday and was buried on Saturday.

I saw where Marty Marion is now coaching the Seminary baseball team. I had a letter from Fred and he sent along a clipping about Marion's accepting his new position. He surely can't hurt the team any. Also, just his name should bring out some good attendances at the Sem games.

I finally received a Lutheran Layman League paper this past week. One small article mentioned Paul Thoemke's name from Beach. It was an article mentioning the project of the Beach LLL which has erected a large cross on a hill right out of Sentinel Butte.

Warm weather has returned to Cuba in full force. The past week has been mighty uncomfortable. Myself, I'd just as soon string along with 75° temperatures.

I really picked up a good cold Thursday night. Today my throat is so sore I can hardly swallow. Last night, I had the chills and tried to sweat them out. I put a blanket on top of myself, even though the weather was about 90°. Man, I was like a wet rag. It did knock the chills for a loop but my sore throat still remains. I just hope it isn't strep throat. It almost feels like it.

I received my first colored slides last week. There were 20 of them. They all turned out good. From now on, most of my pictures are going to be colored slides.

Yesterday the congregation picked the set of house plans for the parsonage. They didn't quite finish selecting the church plans so will finish that tomorrow (next Sunday, that is). The parsonage is really going to be nice. Will cost about $20,000.

I received my social security card this last week also. Now all my papers are in order until my next pick-pocketing.

Dave

La Habana, Cuba
March 9, 1958

Dear Dad, Ma, and Eunice,

Man, I was really surprised to hear that Uncle Walter had a brain tumor operation. It was evident that something was wrong with him; he just didn't look well. A brain tumor was the last thing I had expected. It's tremendous that he's taking it with such a marvelous attitude. An awful lot of ability and talent will be lying on the sick bed as long he's laid up.

Evidently Aunt Marie did get things straight on Aunt Clara according to Prof. and Mrs. Bretscher. They also said that it was a blood clot that was fatal. I haven't written Roy and Elaine as yet but hope to do so soon. They've been hit very hard but the Bretschers said they're taking it quite well.

As I mentioned last week, I finally received my first issue of the *Lutheran Laymen*. It was a long time in coming but now perhaps they have me on their mailing list.

Things are tense, real, real tense in Cuba tonight. Tomorrow is one day that all Cubans would just as soon not see. It is the anniversary of Batista's revolution six years ago. Everyone has a spine-tingling feeling that tomorrow is the day that Castro will show his power in full force. It's hard to describe the existing feeling. The people aren't talking; they aren't going out at night; they're staying within the shelter of their homes; they're just waiting and waiting.

Many of the American men sent their families back to the States this weekend. The others that didn't have stocked up on canned goods. There's just that air of expectancy hanging like an ominous cloud over everyone.

This week Fidel Castro has succeeded in calling a general strike of all schools, both public and private. We had to close down our school out at Reparto Marti also. It's the first time that all religious schools have also closed. We did conduct Saturday School yesterday. It was a rather odd feeling driving the school bus. Everyone just looked sort of odd at me and the bus full of kids. They knew about the threats that Castro had sent out. I suppose they were wandering what crazy school was remaining open in spite of the threats. I was glad to see that day over.

Rebel activities have really picked up momentum. No longer are they mainly confined to Havana and Oriente Province. Instead, they are now also scattered throughout central Cuba as well. Daily, they are finding more dead bodies along the roadside. Many have a note with one word written on it and placed alongside the bodies. The word is "chavito" which translated into English means "informer". These informers are shot, knifed, and some of them are strung up like mummies. The rebels are hitting them hard.

The rebels have also boldly begun to attack trains, buses and autos. They rob the people and then burn their vehicles. Or even worse, they throw incendiary bombs into open windows of public transportation vehicles.

Batista and his regime must also see the hand-writing on the wall. From a very reliable source (American Embassy), I've heard that Batista and his men have all put their homes up for sale; have cleared visas for their families to the States and have made provision for asylum at the American Embassy. I'd say that when the rafters show signs of crumbling the house is about to fall. That's what the signs indicate when you see the government officials placing their homes up for sale.

This Thursday is also another "red-letter" day in Cuba. It is the day of the ill-fated revolt at the Presidential Palace a year ago. That was the day a milk truck pulled up in front of the palace and suddenly the doors opened and out poured rebels armed with sub-machine guns. There was quite a little bloodshed. So, the Cubans figure if the fireworks don't pop tomorrow, they're bound to pop Thursday. Thus, you can see the tension of the people. They don't know for sure; they just wait and wait.

I am slowly getting over my "Cuban" cold. It was a bad one. Yesterday, I had two coughing spells of about half an hour each. The last one was about 12:30 A.M. this morning. The two of them completely washed me out. This morning I was fighting from succumbing to a coughing spell all through the sermon. It was the most miserable time I've ever spent in the pulpit. Just trying to keep from coughing made me break out in a cold sweat. It was about 90° out besides. As a result, the sweat was rolling off me like rain drops. I guess I must have looked as if I just had come in out of a heavy rain.

By the way, we did have a good attendance at the English services this morning. Thirty-seven attended, which is a high since we changed English services from 11:00 to 9:00. Maybe the Americans will finally accustom themselves to the change.

I have gone quite "Cuban" myself. Last week I bought three Guyabaras. They are a Cuban shirt that you do not tuck in at the waste. They take the place of white-shirts and suit-coats during the summer. As a matter of fact, they are the formal wear for men. They are really great for this hot weather. I'll more than get my use out of them.

I got my first colored slides back last week. Everyone turned out well, all 20 of them. From now on, most of my pictures will be in slides. It'll be something to show and to keep as a souvenir when I get back.

This Saturday, Pastor Gruell leaves for St. Louis to meet with the Mission Board and present the congregation's selection of plans for our new church building. We hope to begin by May 1st at the latest.

Dave

La Habana, Cuba
March 16, 1958

Dear Dad, Ma, and Eunice,

Man, talk about quick decisions one must make when his bishop is out of town. Yesterday afternoon at 1:30 Pastor Gruell left for St. Louis to present the plans for our church to the Mission Board. At ten minutes to five, I received a phone call from the mortuary and they asked me if I could have a funeral at 5:00. Said a Lutheran sailor had died on board ship that was docked in Havana. I told them I'd get down there as soon as possible. I picked up the other vicar and we went down together. Since he had conducted two funerals on the Isle of Pines, he took the service. At 5:45 we were out at the cemetery.

That's one thing, though. Here in Havana, they often give you plenty (10 minutes) of notice for a funeral. The sailor was from Norway. His son worked on the same ship so he was present for the funeral. We had no sure way of knowing whether he was a Christian. All we could do is take their word for it. But such are decisions one must make. The son was supposed to come over to church this afternoon and talk with me. He failed to show up.

Well, the lid hasn't blown off yet. Things are definitely worse. Our constitutional guarantees have been suspended again for 45 days. That means censorship of the press once again. Today's *Miami Herald* had the entire front page cut off. Evidently it really carried some bombshell news about what is going on in Cuba.

Schools are supposed to open tomorrow as usual. Thus, they were closed only for one week, the past week. Should they fail to open, we'll lose our entire English-speaking congregation, of Americans, that is. The families have said that they will return to the States so their children don't miss out on school. There was a rumor that the schools would not open until next fall. I don't know how much truth there is to it.

I have had Dad's and Grandpa's birthday cards for more than two weeks. It'd be just like me to forget to mail them now.

I see where Burdette finally signed his contract for $35,000. That must have been quite a sizeable increase from last year's salary. I also hear that Joey Jay is said to be a right-handed Warren Spahn. Is that correct? It's hard to believe but I've read it in quite a few different magazines and articles. As you remarked in your last letter, Casey Wise was good in winter baseball. You'll recall that I mentioned how good he looked. He was simply tremendous. I saw him play quite a few times. He looked nothing like the Casey Wise of the Cubs. Every time he came up, he hit the ball on a line. Everyone says that's a sure sign of a good hitter. He looked very, very good in Cuban Winter League. I don't know how the Braves ever acquired him. Last I knew he was Cubs property.

Temperatures have cooled off for the past couple of days. No doubt that means they're having cooler weather in the States also. It's very comfortable for me now. None of this hot, muggy weather.

Was glad to hear that you received the $80.00 check. It was undoubtedly a mistake on their part for I said nothing about increasing it. However, it's safe in the bank, that's for sure.

Your query about liking Cuba and wanting to return to it can be answered very simply and very quickly, YES. However, that is not my decision to make. It depends upon where I'm sent at the end of my 4th year.

Dave

P.S. Next Monday we have our regular conference in Havana. The other vicar and I have been assigned a paper on the "Youth of the Church, El Joven de La Iglesia." Man, they must really think my Spanish is good if they really think that I can write that paper and deliver it in Spanish. I doubt if it'll work out that way.

I also had a letter from the "110" society at the Sem which is supporting us. They want Jim and me to work up a story and send in pictures which can be used for a feature article in *This Day Magazine*. I will see what we can do about that. I am not promising a thing.

La Habana, Cuba
March 26, 1958

Dear Dad and Ma,

I better get this letter off tonight yet if I intend to write this week. Our conference really put me behind the eight-ball. I did get my paper done but it wasn't in Spanish.

Tomorrow night I'm preaching in English Lenten Service. Pastor has to go to Boca de la Galafre, so I'm taking over. Just finished my sermon a couple of minutes ago. It's a little after 11:00 p.m. now so I will make this a little short.

I finally received my statements from Stix, Baer, and Fuller. Now I'll be able to fill out my income tax returns. I will make the dead-line by about two weeks. That's shaving it pretty close as far as I'm concerned.

Next week, I will be preaching Good Friday at Hershey. Pastor has services here so I'm the only one free to go to Hershey. By the way, last week I began instructing a Jamaican out at Hershey. He's a little slow all the way round, so it's going to take a great deal of patience.

Yesterday, I ran into a marital problem with one of the families who has been coming to our church. Just finished instruction courses with her last week. In reviewing the material with her yesterday, she told me of her problem. Her husband has become an alcoholic and is spending most of his money on booze. She said she has threatened him with divorce but I doubt that she will go through with it. She knows what the Bible says about it and is too much of a Christian to go against God's will. Things will be rough for a-while but with God's help everything will be straightened out.

I just killed a cock-roach that came in from the outside. It was big enough to take a good-sized bite out of you. Man, these things are real pests here. They come in from the outside and give you all kinds of grief.

Things still haven't made a definite turn one way or the other as far as the weather is concerned. I thought that warm weather was here finally (not that I'm rejoicing in the fact) but last night it really cooled off. A really crazy winter all the way around.

By the way, last Wednesday I had my first funeral. Pastor Gruell had not yet returned from St. Louis so I conducted the funeral of a woman on whom we had been calling since I've been here. I was notified Wednesday morning about it. The funeral was at 4:00 p.m. I had a little time in which to prepare myself. It was more time than the funeral for last Saturday. Just like it. When the bishop leaves, you have two funerals in five days.

Dave

La Habana, Cuba
March 29, 1958

Dear Dad, Ma, and Eunice,

Will really do things right and get two letters off this week. That means you should get two letters (I wonder why?) next week. After all, good things come in pairs.

I have tomorrow free as far as preaching is concerned. I don't know what I did to get the day off but Pastor Gruell said he'd preach. Evidently, he decided I did my preaching at our Thursday evening Lenten service.

I had no idea that Uncle Walter was in that serious a condition. I understood from one of your previous letters that he apparently had come out of the operation okay. It's much better, then, if he doesn't linger long.

Don't know if I mentioned it in my last letter or not but I had my first funeral a week ago this past Wednesday. Pastor had not yet returned from St. Louis so I had the service with only about seven hours-notice to get ready.

I had a nice letter from Grandpa Dissen this past week. He's still the same walking library of information. Man, he quoted me statistics about foreign languages that I'd never be able to remember. He has an amazing and very active and alert mind, even at his ripe old age. It's simply fabulous that he continues the way he does. He's a real marvel.

I also heard from Walt last week. Apparently, he is satisfied with his new position. Even though he is low man on the totem pole, if I know him, he won't be for very long. Probably in five years or so he'll be head of his company.

From what we hear and read on this island, the U.S. is in a very shaky and critical economic condition. If so, only the people themselves are to blame. Whenever they hear the word "depression," they immediately tighten up and hold on to their money. If there's anything that brings on a depression, it's that very reaction. Let the people keep circulating what they have and things will be able to continue in a proper cycle. But start putting the bite on the wallet and everything will hit the skids.

This past week I heard from a rather reliable source that Ken Fischer (one of my seminary room-mates) is now engaged. Perhaps that explains why I haven't had any answers to my correspondence. He's been too tied up with his gal. He certainly had a good opportunity for meeting his future Frau since he is working with about 10,000 college students. He is vicaring as a student campus pastor at Oregon University.

What's new in the political situation of Cuba? You have to keep us posted now as we once again have censorship. Only info we get is mouth to mouth. I do know, though, that all airplane flights were cancelled to Santiago de Cuba in Oriente Province for several days last week. Things were in control of the rebels and plane flights were not safe. I also heard that a large number of Batista's soldiers defected to Castro in Oriente Province. A close source of information to the Presidential Palace (one of the young men taking instruction for membership) told me yesterday that this coming week is the week in which Castro intends to call for a general strike throughout Cuba. If effective, it means one thing: "Good-bye Batista!" Of all weeks, he'd have to pick Holy Week. Next Saturday is supposed to be the day. Time will tell. You get so used to hearing things that you think they will never happen.

Tomorrow, I may go out to the Hershey Golf Course with Pastor Gruell in the afternoon and get in a few swings. I haven't been out in over a month now. Last time I shot a 55 in nine holes. I hope to improve that if possible.

I learned only the other day that the family which lives two houses down and on the other side of the street from the church has a pet lion in their backyard plus many other animals. Maybe one of these days I'll take a safari and snap a couple of pictures of it.

Baseball will soon be opening for another season. It appears that Milwaukee and St. Louis will be battling it out, with San Francisco also making a bid. St. Louis very definitely is going to be tough, there's no getting around it. The Kasko and Dark shift will help tremendously.

Dave

9

APRIL 1958

La Habana, Cuba
April 6, 1958

Dear Dad and Ma, and Eunice,

We had a fairly good attendance at our Easter English service this morning. Fifty-three were present for that service. We also had sunrise service at 6:30, only 18 were present for that service. In our regular 11:00 Spanish service we had 19 in attendance. Pastor did the preaching in all three services. Why, I don't know, but he can't complain about not having someone to help him out.

Things look as if I may be coming home about the 10th of August or so. I received a letter yesterday from Ken Fischer informing me that he is engaged and getting married on August 17th in Eugene, Oregon. He wants all of us in his wedding party. If things work out, we should be able to pile into someone's car and take off in a group, greatly saving on expenses. I haven't decided certainly that I'm going but as of now I see nothing that should stop me. Though I hadn't planned on leaving Havana until about the 18th of August, Pastor Gruell said he would not object to my leaving the 10th.

Everything is yet quiet in Havana, even though Fidel was supposed to wage all-out war at midnight last night. Life is fairly normal but fear is still there. All traffic coming into Havana is thoroughly checked. Police cars, soldiers and SIM (Secret Police) are stationed thick and heavy throughout the main thorough fares. You really get a taste of what living is like in a county which is about to undergo an all-out revolution. No security at all. Arms and force are the rule of the day.

On Good Friday, I preached out at Hershey, even though quite a few of the people begged me not to go out. They were afraid things might start popping and I'd get caught somewhere along the way. I told them there was nothing to fear as Fidel had said he wouldn't start anything until the 5th at midnight. Naturally, it was also a talking point to maybe talk me out of the fact that I should not go. As it was, when I got out there the members had everything ready so I could have services immediately and get back to Havana as quickly as possible.

This past week we accepted into Communicant membership my first adult confirmand. Pastor Gruell was present for the private examination and she came through with flying colors. I think that she's really going to be a sound Christian and a blessing to many. She's really well indoctrinated.

Not much more to say. Would like to know what my bank account on the State Side is now with this last check of $80.00 you received from the Mission Board. I haven't the slightest idea. After all, I don't want to get too much money in the bank, right Dad?

Dave

P.S. Where was your last week's letter? Probably come tomorrow.

La Habana, Cuba
April 19, 1958

Dear Dad and Ma,

Not too much this week as time is very short and precious. With conference coming up next week, I'll have my hands full.

I had hoped to work on my sermon for next Sunday (the 27th) sometime this week but things just didn't materialize. Last night was especially set aside for that purpose and then I ended up going out to Hershey to preach. The other vicar was sick and couldn't make it. Hence, I automatically drew the assignment.

Things have really been upset in the Gruell household this week. Monday night their little Mary (2 years) was taken into the clinic with a 104 ½ temperature. Overnight it climbed to 106°. Wednesday it finally dropped off some. Doctors say it is an acute attack of colitis. She was in critical condition for three days and is finally starting to pull out of it. Believe me, it's really hard to see the little gal lying on the bed practically lifeless. We will all be happy and thankful if the Good Lord restores her to the healthy, happy girl she was before.

Monday morning at 9:45 we fly to Miami and then drive the remainder of the way. Leave again Friday afternoon by plane for Havana. I sure hope I can do some sermon work during the week. Otherwise, wow! I just hate to think of it.

I doubt if I'll be going to Fischer's wedding. I had decided that when I heard from Wille. He doesn't think he'll be going and if he doesn't go, we won't have a ride. At least to my knowledge, we wouldn't.

We had a wonderfully refreshing cool spell this week. The past four days have been marvelous. However, tomorrow the hot weather is forecast to return. Sounds as if happy days are here again!

Enclosed you'll find a piece of my handiwork. I decided to put out an all-English bulletin and Pastor Gruell will be putting out an all-Spanish bulletin.

We heard from the Mission Board that they have applied for two vicars for Havana again. One to do Spanish work at Reparto Marti and the other to do English and German work in our congregation here.

Dave

La Habana, Cuba
April 28, 1958

Dear Dad, Ma, and Eunice,

Well, I don't know why you had the charges reversed on that long distance phone call but I guess that's your business. After all, you're supposed to be in a recession in the States. That meant that the $5.00 worth of change which I had with me in the phone booth just added that much more weight to my pockets. Thanks for picking up the tab. I will make it up when August rolls around.

By the way, Eunice, I did try to call Fred. As a matter of fact, I tried three times. Finally, at 12:20 a.m. I gave up. They said he had gone to the library. That boy really must study late. Of course, the time in Oshkosh was only 11:20, so I guess that isn't too late at that. However, I wasn't about to stay up any longer as I had only had three hours of sleep the previous night. We stayed up playing canasta until midnight and then had to get up at 3:00 and take off for Lakeland.

We arrived back in Havana Saturday morning about 10:00, which was unscheduled. We had planned to leave Miami Friday night at 9:50 but when we got back around 7:00 and called for reservations we found that this particular flight had been cancelled for the past month. Thus, we had to sit over in Miami Friday night and leave Saturday morning at 8:00.

By the way, Friday night while we were laying over, we went out bowling. My first time in over a year. In my first game, I hit 158 and the second game I hit 128. I didn't think that was too bad considering things. I was really rusty!

Saturday naturally was one busy mad-house for me. I had my sermon to prepare and my bulletin to put out. However, I did manage to get everything done. I don't want too many more days like it, though. Otherwise, I'll be developing an ulcer before I'm out of the twenties.

I did quite a bit of shopping on this trip to Miami. Monday afternoon we went out and really did up the town. I bought a new Samsonite Magnesium coated suitcase for $30.00 plus tax. I also picked up several pair of wash and wear slacks, socks, and shoes. I spent enough for a-while. I just wanted to do my share in getting the economy stronger again.

Last Wednesday afternoon we had our radio interview, which lasted about ten minutes. I understand that it was broadcast to quite a few of the Latin American countries. Several of our people picked it up from South American broadcasts. We also had an interview with the United Press correspondent. Naturally, you can guess what they were mainly interested in, the political situation. However, we gave them a full load on our mission work and tried to evade their political questions as much as possible. It was the best policy considering the law that Batista just passed about taking care of those who talk about the situation.

Things are rather quiet in Cuba today. As I said several weeks ago, Batista has had it. He's almost washed up as of now. It's only a matter of time before he'll be forced to surrender or pull up stakes. Just as good.

Next Monday Pastor Gruell and his family go on their vacation. They'll be gone the month of May. By the way, he purchased a Nash Rambler Station Wagon the other week and it's really a tremendous little car. I didn't realize Nash put out anything that good.

Dave

P.S. The Sundays of the 17th and 24th of August sound okay. I don't believe that I'll be going to Fischer's wedding. Wille isn't going so that means no ride. I can spend the time just as well and profitably by taking off some place with you and Ma. I should be home about the 20th of August.

10

MAY 1958

La Habana, Cuba
May 6, 1958

Dear Dad and Ma, and Eunice,

Things are in full swing for me as of yesterday. Pastor Gruell and family left on schedule yesterday. They will not return until May 31st. I must try to keep things for our church in Cuba alive and well until he returns. I will have plenty to keep me occupied.

I had a nice letter from Fred yesterday. He informed me that you had been fishing. As we expected, he said that Dad took great delight in catching a sheep head. He said that Dad was planning on taking it back home and mounting it! A real trophy! Funny, I never heard anything in Dad's letter about it. Oh well, so fish stories go.

Your suggestion as to the 17th and 24th of August sounds like a fabulous idea. Have no idea where you plan to go on your vacation but I'm game for it. (Havana, Cuba?). It will be good for all of us to get out some place and do a little relaxing. This includes the school teacher also if she isn't too busy filling her brain with knowledge.

Last Saturday we took in two more communicant members. Man, it is a real thrill to see how wonderfully the Holy Spirit works through adult instruction classes when His Word is used. I started with this couple last fall and finished with them last Thursday night. Saturday was their examination. She had been a former Roman Catholic. The joy that possessed her as she answered the questions and confessed her faith in her Savior is simply indescribable. I will really miss my Thursday night discussions with them for they were very lively and interesting.

Things sort of faded out on the immediate construction of the parsonage. When it came time to sign the contract last week, it fizzled. The contractor wanted us to sign everything, but he wanted to sign nothing. No soap on such a deal as this. Now we'll wait until Pastor returns from his vacation before anything more is done.

I see where those Cubs really gave the Braves a rocking. Man, the way they look now they could be dangerous. I don't know where all their power came from but they surely have been swinging a powerful bat. Aaron had better start coming around soon. He hasn't done much at all. Roach seems to be okay. I can't understand why Casey Wise hasn't been used. Given a chance, he should go all the way. I just hope the Braves don't lose their rights on him.

So much for now. It's only 9:00 a.m. but it's so hot out that I'm roasting in my room. Much more of this pleasant weather to which to look forward.

Dave

La Habana, Cuba
May 12, 1958

Dear Dad, Ma, and Eunice,

Got a little letter writing to do so better get at least one off yet tonight.

Today was my day of leisure and it turned out to be just that except for the adult instruction class I just had this evening. Jim (the other vicar) and I went to see the Capitol Building this afternoon. We saw the outside (which we had seen many times) but they wouldn't let us inside. The guards gave us a rather cold shoulder. They told us to come back another day. Evidently, they must have been having some kind of meeting today and didn't want sightseers inside the building.

One week has passed since Pastor and family left on vacation. So far, we've been doing okay on meals. Gruell's maid is working for us this month. She's doing our cooking and laundry. I must say that she can cook far better than I thought she'd be able to. She makes the best French-fries I've eaten in a long time. Also fixed some delicious chicken today. They've had a special on ice cream at one of the grocery stores (3 pints for $1.00) so our desserts have been ice cream and cookies. The maid does not know how to fix desserts, so we have to make out on canned desserts.

Tomorrow I have to take care of trading $2,500 in American checks for Cuban money and then deposit it in the church's account. Whenever we receive checks for large amounts, we sell them to a Cuban businessman if possible. This saves us paying ½ of 1% for cashing the checks. It also saves the Cuban businessman who has a State-side account of having to pay to get his Cuban money changed into American money. It's a vicious circle but it's the only way to do it. Otherwise, both people lose out and the only one who makes anything on it is the bank.

Last week was rather hectic but this week I hope to have my schedule so arranged that my added responsibilities will be more balanced. It's good disciplinary practice, that's for sure.

By the way, I noticed in the *Lutheran Witness* that the N.D. polio poster girl is a Hofstad girl from our former New Rockford church. I don't recall the name. Does Dad? Very likely a new family.

Monsoon season has once again arrived. We can expect much rain now until next October. We really have had a lot of water in the past two days. It makes the weather unpleasantly hot and muggy. How I love it???

I see where the Braves have been doing themselves right proud. Let them continue the way they have in the past week and I won't complain. I see where the Cards are beginning to make their move. They'll be tough from now on in.

Dave

P.S. Evidently, we're not getting our vicar for Havana this coming year from St. Louis. I had a list of the vicarage assignments and no one from the Sem was headed for Cuba. I suppose it will be a Springfield man. Or it could be, too, that they're calling a full-time pastor for work in Havana. That would be by far the best. It would eliminate the necessity of having to break in a new vicar every year.

One question for Dad: How large is the communicant membership in Union Grove now? Have meant to ask this for some time but keep forgetting it! I've always figured it to be about 225 or so. Please let me know!

La Habana, Cuba
May 18, 1958

Dear Dad and Ma,

I was glad to hear that the right person took the money out of the Mother's Day card. The way Dad played it up you'd think he was writing a murder mystery with the thrilling climax not revealed until the very end. However, when he dragged it out as long as he did, I figured it would turn out with an "and they lived happily ever after" ending. I wasn't disappointed, either.

I'm listening right now to some good American records on the radio. I figure I may as well get my money out of the radio which I put into it this past week. All six tubes went bad on it. It cost me about $14.00 to repair it. I would not have had the work done on it but it does belong to one of our members who is letting me enjoy it while I'm down here.

That deep-freeze sounds okay. Perhaps the members could now take a hint (subtle, naturally) and help you fill it. I know you wouldn't mind that one bit.

I heard from the Gruell's this past week. They're enjoying their vacation tremendously. They said the States is really a welcome change. Too bad he has only one month's vacation. After putting up with me for nine months, the Mission Board should have given him half a year???

I reckon the cabin plan at Oshkosh will be okay. I had thought perhaps we could make a partial swing out West once again but perhaps that wouldn't go over too big. I would like to see a few of the old places where we lived. Of course, there's so much I'd like to crowd into those few weeks it can't all be done. I understand that classes at the Sem will start about September 1st this year. They're under a new system now and the school year begins much earlier.

A week ago, the assignments were handed out at the Sem. Apparently Cuba isn't getting as much as even one vicar this year. They say it's because of the political situation (rumor which I heard from one of the fellas at the Sem). It surely is a shame because workers are needed very badly this particular time in Cuba. I pity poor Pastor Gruell. He's literally swamped with work now and no help next year will make him fit to be tied.

I'm enclosing one of the write-ups I made for the Havana Post, the only daily English newspaper in Havana. They've been very cooperative in giving us newspaper space.

So much for now. The two of us bachelors are still making out okay. One word of parting advice, someone put a hex on the Cardinals. They're starting to snowball now just a little too fast.

Dave

La Habana, Cuba
May 26, 1958

Dear Dad, Ma, and Eunice

I finally have a clear morning once again. Last week from Thursday through Saturday we really had rain. It was very good duck weather, that's for sure.

Yesterday, our church attendance took another dip. It dropped down to 25 in English. I guess that can be expected for the great build-up next week. Why do I say that? Next Sunday will be the first Sunday Pastor Gruell is back from vacation. That means the church should be practically full. After all, the people who have been on vacation on the past three Sundays should be back to make a good impression on Pastor when he returns.

We had a real beautiful afternoon yesterday. Not so much weather wise but recreational wise. Vicar Sudbrock and I ate dinner at one of our Cuban member's homes. Then we went out to Playa del Santa Maria (Santa Maria Beach) for an afternoon of swimming in the Ocean. Santa Maria del Mar is another one of these private affairs. You need a pass to get in but this family had one. Man, it's simply fabulous to let these big rolling waves hit you and sweep you right along. The beach is very beautiful. It has just gorgeous sand. It's not as big as Varadero Beach but it is still fabulous. Mr. Sudbrock and I may go out again today since we always take Mondays as our day off. This family said we could use their pass whenever we wanted. Fabulous! Fabulous! Fabulous! Fabulous! That's the only way I can describe this beach and swimming in the Atlantic.

Yesterday we had a visitor at our services. Turned out that he will be a permanent fixture in our congregation. He was a young man from New York who is working as Assistant Treasurer for Esso Company in Havana. His family is to come down in about three weeks. He is a real swell young man. He knew several of the vicars that had served in his congregation in New York whom I knew. I am supposed to go out to supper with him sometime this week.

We also had another American visitor yesterday. After services, I was talking with him and asked him what line of business he was in in the States. He replied, hesitatingly, uh, uh, the liquor business. He's from Louisville, Kentucky so I guess he's in the right spot for it.

I see where the Braves traded Hazle off to the Tigers. I sure hope that trade doesn't fizzle. After all, Hazle really wasn't with them too long; not long enough to give him a real chance. I hope they get a good replacement for him. They'll need something in the line of hitting to overtake San Francisco. The Giants really have power this year.

Dave

11

JUNE 1958

La Habana, Cuba
June 1, 1958

Dear Dad and Ma,

I'm slowly recuperating from the fabulous time I had on that fabulous beach last Monday. Sunday, I suffered no effects from the sun at all. Monday was a different story. We were only out for about an hour. For me, it was half an hour too long. I started peeling yesterday and am really clipping it off today. Funny thing was, I never blistered until Thursday. Perhaps the great humidity here had something to do with that. At any rate, the next time I'll watch myself a little more.

I had complete charge of services yet this Sunday. Last Tuesday, I had a telegram from Pastor Gruell reading: "Arriving Tuesday, June 3." In other words, he was politely telling me that I'd also be preaching today. Ordinarily, I wouldn't have. First Sunday of the month is communion Sunday. On that Sunday, Pastor Gruell spells me. Otherwise, I generally take all the other Sundays.

I was not aware of the fact that Walt was graduating June 8th. I haven't heard a thing from him in the last month or so. I was under the impression that he had graduated in March already. I hope I can find some kind of decent card for him.

I haven't heard from Bill and Marilyn in quite some time now either. I don't know if Bill has been re-hired or not? One thing about Grandpa Dissen! He at least answers my letters. He's really on the ball for his age, believe me.

We're still keeping our fingers crossed in the hopes that Havana will receive a vicar. We've heard nothing definite as yet. I don't know what Pastor Gruell will do if they don't come through for him.

We're just sitting and waiting with our building program now until Pastor Gruell returns. The church plans are final (subject to his change) and we're now waiting for the contractors to start bidding. Naturally, this must be done while he is here.

I see where the Braves have momentarily regained first place. For how long, who knows? I was surprised to see Hazle go, there's no doubt about that. Also, I see where Philipps is doing okay for himself. Paine also. I figured they would. Aaron has been a big disappointment. I can't figure him out. Covington continues to be a pleasant surprise. They need someone to carry them along. What happened to Schoendienst! I notice he hasn't played in the last several games.

Dave

P.S. Enclosed is one of our Sunday service write-ups in the only daily English paper in Havana, the Havana Post. They have been very gracious in giving us space considering the owners are Catholic.

La Habana, Cuba
June 10, 1958

Dear Dad and Ma,

Time is really slipping by fast. Here it is, Tuesday morning already and still no letter written. I had better remedy that situation before it's too late.

Sunday afternoon Pastor Gruell and wife, Mr. Sudbrock, and I were invited out to the home of the Society Editor of the Havana Post in honor of her daughter who had just returned from college in the States. Many others were also present. We were rather surprised to receive the invitation because after all, she's Baptist. However, she said she was so impressed with our Sunday service write-ups that she wanted her daughter to meet these fine Christian young men at the church. The invitation was quite unexpected, to say the least. I guess it does show, though, that Christ-centered write-ups in a daily newspaper do get through to some people. May be invited out there again in the near future for a supper. That wouldn't be too bad, since the daughter is a very pleasant young gal.

Yesterday morning, we went out to the Rover's Club for a little respite from the heat. Their swimming pool is really nice. Only one thing wrong. I still haven't found a way to combat the rays of old man sun. The sun did a nice job of painting my back red again. I suppose I'll be peeling in about three or four days. I just can't seem to take a tan.

This coming Saturday will have enough hair-raising episodes to write a book about (I believe). We plan to take the Saturday School children on a closing picnic and devotional service. Apparently, it will be out at Hershey Gardens (a drive of about 30 miles). I draw the pleasant task of manipulating the school bus. With a screaming load of young children confined on that bus ride for about 2 ½ hours, I think I'll be fit to be tied by the time we get out there. It really isn't as bad as all that, but man, they do wear on your nerves at times.

Last night, Pastor Gruell was to find out definitely who will be building the house. I haven't heard yet from him this morning. Anyway, he plans to break ground definitely for the parsonage this week. The church is still about a month or more away.

I heard yesterday from this one family in St. Louis that they plan to come down to Cuba in July. It will be good to see them again. I knew them from Holy Cross Lutheran. They're members there. He's a baker. His daughter is a nurse at Lutheran Hospital. She is one of Fischer's old flames.

May Dad have a very, very Happy Father's Day by seeing the Braves start out on a 15-game winning streak. They need it.

Dave

Dear Dad, Ma, and Eunice,

We had a very successful picnic for our Saturday School children this past Saturday morning. The weather held out beautifully. We were rather worried about it because last Tuesday, Wednesday, and Thursday we had solid, steady rain. Saturday was wonderful, though. We had a very nice park in which to eat our lunch. We played most of our games on the athletic field of one of the new schools.

Then to top things off, when we returned from the picnic, Pastor Gruell had tremendous news waiting in the form of a letter from the Mission Board. Havana is receiving two more workers. They are not vicars. Both of them are studying and preparing for colloquies. One is an ex-Catholic priest from Ecuador (whom I know from the Sem) and the other is a German worker from Germany. Believe me, that will alleviate much pressure from Pastor Gruell. It means another Spanish man, in addition to the German man. We will now have English, German and Spanish services. When they're coming, we do not know. The good news in itself will satisfy until their arrival.

Sunday afternoon, we all went out to a finca about 120 kilometers from Havana. It was right in the mountains in Pinar del Rio Province. Very beautiful. I took about 10 color pictures and then ran out of film. I plan to take the roll of film down for developing today. I sure wish I would have had more film. On this finca they had the most gorgeous flowers you've ever seen.

Monday morning, we made our usual trip out to the Rover's Club for a morning of swimming. For the first time, I got up enough courage to try diving. They weren't the best executed dives but I did manage to come up again. I had my regular bout with the sun, too. This time I used PFI powder for my sunburn. I was pleasantly surprised with the relief it gave me. It wasn't perhaps the best medicine for it, but it sure was better than nothing.

Yesterday, they finally began construction on Pastor's parsonage. He signed the final contract last Friday. They have three months in which to put the house up. Thereafter, the construction company is penalized for every day they run over.

I see no reason why I wouldn't be able to preach before I leave for the Sem. I doubt if it would be more than two Sundays though, because I believe the Sem begins about September 5th.

I can't say that I'm too pleased with Haney's performance. Any manager who leaves a pitcher in as long as Spahn was left in against the Cubs should have his head examined. It was an outrage to let Chicago knock him around for nine runs.

Dave

Dear Dad, Ma, and Eunice,

The trip to Bill and Marilyn's rings okay with me. I had a letter from Marilyn yesterday in which she stated they were hoping we would stay for more than a day or two. I don't know how well that would work? I do want to see them, though. Maybe we could still spend three or four days at a cabin. That remains to be seen.

Friday evening when I arrived at Hershey, I learned that one of the men who had been attending services was in critical condition from a stroke. He had been speechless and unconscious for a week. I had a devotion with him and he showed signs of understanding. After services, the entire group walked over to his house. We had a short meditation for him and then joined in chain prayer for him.

Yesterday morning, Pastor Gruell received a telegram informing him that the man had died. We went out in the afternoon to see the survivors and make arrangements for the funeral (which we figured would be today). Lo and behold, when we got close to their house, we saw the hearse standing in front of it and people clustered all about. We arrived fifteen minutes before the funeral. Both of us had on guayaberas instead of suits but Pastor Gruell conducted the service anyway. If they had they let us know in the telegram that the funeral was yesterday we could have been prepared. All the telegram said was: "Wilson dead." You must agree, it's not too informing.

Pastor Gruell has done some talking about going down to the southern end of the island on his annual mission scouting tour before Mr. Sudbrock and I leave. He may take his car and then the three of us would go together. It would mean leaving on a Monday and coming back on Saturday. I would sure go for that. It would give me a wonderful opportunity to see practically the entire island.

Ma shouldn't feel too bad about taking naps in the afternoon. I have gotten into the habit since I've been down here. In Cuba, all activity slows down to a crawl between 12:00 and 3:00 every day. In this period, I generally manage to get about 30 to 45 minutes of shut-eye every day. If you don't, you really feel washed out about midnight.

I had another enjoyable day (morning) at the Rover's Club yesterday. I'm finally getting to the point where only my shoulders get sunburned. I may pull through yet.

Our VBS will not be conducted until the first two weeks in August. That means I'll be ready for a vacation by the time I get home.

Dave

La Habana, Cuba
June 29, 1958

Dear Dad and Ma,

This afternoon we have before us the job of collecting all the VBS material which has been translated from English into Spanish. You can imagine the work involved just in the translation alone. Pastor Gruell did all the translation. The rest of us helped in the drawings of pictures, etc. While I'm on the topic of VBS, we'd appreciate it very much if you would send us the devotional topics for this year's VBS material. We did not receive any Senior department material. Hence, we have no devotional topics. The faster the better, if you're willing to part with your Senior Manual.

We had rather good attendances in our services this morning. English numbered 33 and Spanish 25. Spanish has been picking right up. However, I "joke" with Pastor Gruell that he is sheep-stealing from me. Last week he had eight members from my English list in his Spanish service. Today he had five. This week I'm confirming one adult who was in Spanish service today. Pastor let me know that he would like to have this family in his Spanish service. The most important thing is that they are in church period, whether that be in the English or Spanish service.

Believe it or not, I saw my first Brave's game on TV yesterday afternoon. I watched every bit of it except for some of the first inning. I wasn't too impressed. What the Braves badly need is some hitting. They have good pitching but the pitchers also need some runs if they are going to win. Willey looked very good. I was disappointed at Haney, though, for letting Willey stay in when his control went bad in the ninth. Complete games aren't that important. Do you realize what that takes out of a pitcher when he has to throw so many pitches? Why not put in a relief pitcher? The important thing is to win! I plan to watch the Braves and Pirates next week. That is the game of the week. And Cuba TV now has the game of the week beamed into the country.

I just happened to think that July 27th my driver's license expires. If you have my application blank, would you please send it to me immediately? They'll probably send it to me at home. I plan to write them today and ask them to send the application blank to me in Cuba. I don't want my license to expire on me.

I reckon that our planned trip to Santiago de Cuba has been shattered. Political conditions are anything but peaceful down in the southern sector. Castro is still causing plenty of trouble. You don't hear much about it because everything is censored. However, the American Embassy in Havana advised us against such a trip. They said there were no guarantees on safe conduct. It seems as if this is the wrong year in Cuba for seeing all of the island.

I found out that last week I forgot to place stamps on your letter. That's very likely why you didn't hear from me. The postman informed me of it yesterday.

I must go to work on collating that material now. More next week.

Dave

12

JULY 1958

La Habana, Cuba
July 6, 1958

Dear Dad and Ma,

Thanks for the enclosure of my driver's license renewal blank. That had me personally worried. It's now in the mail. I hope that they send it to me via air mail. I included the air mail in the check. That's the only way I'll get my license here before my present one expires. If I don't have my new license by the 27th, I suppose it means no driving, (legally, that is).

Today is the 12th wedding anniversary of Pastor Gruell and his wife. Mr. Sudbrock (the other vicar) and I are taking them out for dinner tonight Cuban style. By Cuban style, I mean that we will eat about 10:30 or 11:00 tonight. We certainly hope that they have many more anniversaries. They're a tremendous Christian couple. They've done so much for me and I know Mr. Sudbrock will second that.

This morning we took in two new members to our congregation. One was in our English congregation and the other in our Spanish. I finished up with the English communicant only last night. He is a Spaniard by birth but speaks fluent English. Being a Spaniard, he was naturally a Catholic. But he's now a solid Lutheran Christian. He's going to be a tremendous asset to this congregation. Now we pray that his wife will soon join him. She's still R.C. but she admits that there is nothing she can find wrong in our teaching on the basis of Scripture. She also sees the errors of R.C. Yet, she fears what her friends and family will say if she converts to Lutheranism. We're sure she'll eventually join as a member with her husband, but it will take a little more time.

Tomorrow night we have a very important meeting of both our English and Spanish congregations. We're taking a semi-annual examination of our stewardship policy and general church program. It's very necessary for all of us. We hope that we have a good attendance. All tomorrow afternoon Pastor and I will be in conference for the meeting. He's going to take charge of the Spanish group and I'll have charge of the English.

Last Wednesday Pastor Karl arrived on schedule. He's an older man of about 42 or 43. Needless to say, he has some idiosyncrasies. I've learned a few since I've been with him so much of the time. I've been showing him around and bringing him to the homes of the German speaking people. I'm sure he will work out okay, though.

I knew the results of last week's Saturday game. I saw it on TV. Sad to say, I also saw the results of the Braves-Pirates game on TV this last Saturday. Schoendienst looked like a little kid playing in his first game. Unless the Braves get a little enthusiasm, they're out of it. I've never seen such a lifeless team, even if I do have to say it of my Braves. They need some power, life and energy.

You will not receive a check from the Mission Board for me this month. Pastor Gruell forgot to tell them to deduct it. Hence, next month I plan to have them send you $160.00 or $180.00

Dave

La Habana, Cuba
July 26, 1958

Dear Dad and Ma,

Thanks for the beautiful birthday card. It arrived today. I'll be more than content to wait until I arrive home. All that I expect, and that which I will be more than satisfied with, will be some home-made ice cream waiting for me in the deep freeze. I hope that request can be filled.

So far as we know, things have been very quiet in Cuba today. As you well know, last July 26th is when Fidel Castro tried his attempted revolution and he failed. It was expected that Castro's 26th of July Movement would make things a little hot today. Our one member, who is 1st vice-consul in the American Embassy, was sent down to our Embassy building in Santiago de Cuba this week. The political situation down there got so out of hand that they (the Embassy department) requested Mr. Geerken's help this week. I hope he is back by now. If not, he may get in on some unpleasant 26th of July memories.

WELL, WE'RE FINALLY DOING IT, THE WAY IT APPEARS NOW. NEXT WEEK WE PLAN TO HAVE GROUND BREAKING CEREMONIES FOR OUR NEW CHURCH. If everything works out okay, we'll hold the ceremonies at 3:00 next Sunday afternoon. Before I leave, I may get to see the first phase of work done on our church. I sure wish I could be here when it is dedicated. It'll be simply fabulously beautiful, and all for a cost of $75,000 complete. That price, by the way, includes air-conditioning. Believe me, air conditioning will be wonderful.

Tuesday morning I'll be sending my trunk and suit-case of books to Wally's shop in St. Louis. Luckily, I have a friend who is in the customs business in Havana. He's taking care of all the red-tape and papers for me.

I don't suppose I'll get too much done this week. A family I know from St. Louis will be coming into Havana Tuesday evening. I'll be with them a day or two. Wednesday, Mr. Sudbrock's girl-friend is coming in. I'll get in some sightseeing with them since both of us have only a short time remaining in which to do it. Thursday morning, Pastor Gruell and his wife, Mr. Sudbrock and his gal, and I are going up to Varadero Beach for the day. We'll make the most of those days next week, for so far I've done very little sightseeing in Cuba. And time has about run out.

I can't say that I would turn down the idea of spending some time at a cottage near Oshkosh. I think it's tremendous. And for the sake of repetition, I'll be leaving Havana the 15th or 16th of August. Our VBS closes the 15th of August, so I may not be able to leave yet that day. If I do leave the 15th of August, Dad and I have a meeting place at County Stadium for that doubleheader on the 16th. Ma is also invited if she can stand to sit through this wonderful sporting event!

This time you should receive a check of $160.00 from the Mission Board. That is the amount I told them to send you. Trust that Ma has a record of my state-side bank account. I have somewhat of a record. But how accurate, I don't know. Both Walt and Bill burned up checks that I sent them. Hence, that throws more confusion into the picture. However, when I see them, I'll remind them that a gift is a gift and should be accepted as such.

I will definitely leave Cuba with the blessing (?) of all the German members in our congregation. In the three weeks which Pastor Karl (our new German vicar) has been here, the German members have made it very clear to him that I was far too rough on them in expecting to see the fruits of their Christianity, and that included their regular attendance in church. They complained to him that I never gave them any peace and rest; that I was always calling on them. Now, after I'm gone, they'll have some time in which to catch their second breath.

By the way, last week we had a real "beauty queen" in our services. Her name was Nancy Showman, a girl from Maryland. She and her mother were given a two weeks-vacation in Havana as part of her "Title" prize. She was selected as "Miss Apple Blossom Queen of the U.S."

So much for this time. You can start making that good old-fashioned home-made ice cream now. And keep your cotton-picking hands off it until I get in a lick or two or three or four!

Dave

P.S.   There is no need for any exegesis on Dad's question. When you come to love your work and the people among whom you work, you leave much of yourself behind when you depart. Simple as that! ABC. Yes, I have loved my vicarage in Cuba!

Holy Trinity Lutheran Church, Havana, Cuba.
Once considered by many to be the most beautiful building
in Cuba, it was converted into a warehouse and later
included as part of a planetarium under Fidel Castro.

EPILOGUE

My vicarage in Cuba ended at the beginning of August, 1958. When I left Cuba, the members of Holy Trinity Lutheran Church in Havana had just broken ground for the construction of their new church, funded by a generous contribution of $50,000 from the Lutheran Woman's Missionary League of the LCMS.

There was much opportunity for missionary work on this narrow, approximately 780-mile-long and 120-mile-wide island of about five million people at that time. Our three congregations were in Havana; in Central Hershey near Havana; and in Boca de Galafre, about 130 miles southwest of Havana. I was privileged to assist in all three congregations. Holy Trinity served Cubans, Americans, and Europeans from all over Havana. The congregation members in Central Hershey were primarily Jamaican. Our mission work faced numerous challenges that came from the gambling, vice, political corruption, materialism, and religious indifference that was so prevalent.

After the Battle of Santa Clara on January 1, 1959, led by Che Guevara, who had joined Fidel Castro's revolution, the Dictatorship of Fulgencio Batista came to an end. Early on January 1, 1959, Batista fled to the Dominican Republic. From there, he went to Portugal and ended up dying from a heart attack in Spain.

On January 8, 1959, Fidel and his 26th of July Revolutionary Movement entered Havana in a victory celebration. Religious freedom soon ended, along with other freedoms. Missionary Gruell and his family eventually relocated to Miami, Florida, where Pastor Gruell continued a Spanish ministry which included some members from the Havana congregation who also fled from Cuba.

People ask, "What happened to the new Lutheran Church that was erected in 1959 – the church which Cubans at that time called "the most beautiful building on the island?" Rev. Herman Glienke, who had been a missionary in Cuba and the Isle of Pines (1952-1961), learned what happened when he interviewed an anonymous woman, who with her husband and three

127

children, arrived in the United States on a Freedom Flight in 1972 (*The Lutheran Woman's Quarterly*, Vol. XXX1, No. 3, of Summer 1973).

This woman told Pastor Glienke that the church was converted into a warehouse. The towering cross was removed. Why? The answer was: "Here we have nothing but Fidel's word; we don't need anything from God." The church later became part of a planetarium that was built next to the church. The new parsonage served as the living quarters for the director of the planetarium.

Under the rule of Communism, parents lost control over their children. At age five, children were sent to government nurseries for 15 days or more at a time. Freedom came to an end. All decisions were made for the people. Atheists were almost the only satisfied people.

Many Christians and others were arrested, thrown into prison, and frequently executed by a firing squad. At this time, the pastor husband of this anonymous woman added that he had been arrested and spent three years in prison, during which time he was trying to leave the country legally. He said that one night while he and the other prisoners were asleep on the concrete floor that they were awakened by a terrible noise. They were told more prisoners were being executed. Within a matter of seconds, they heard an imprisoned pastor cry out: "Viva Cristo Rey!" (Long live Christ the King!). This was followed by a shout. Then complete silence. A few days later, another man, who was a religious prisoner, shouted: "Cuba, wake up!" Shots were heard. Then there was nothing but quiet.

Periodically, I still think about all the persecution and bloodshed that were experienced by Christians and others who were political prisoners under Cuban Communism. They endured immense suffering, hardships, and oppression.

As I reflect on my vicarage in Cuba and see what is happening in our country in 2021, it seems to me that much of what is going on now is a WAKE-UP CALL to ALL Americans. Today we thank God for the freedoms that we still enjoy in the United States! But how long will we enjoy them? America is backsliding more and more from God and the saving truths of His Word. A poll in March of 2021 indicated that only 47% of Americans claim to be members of a church. We Americans need to repent daily of our sins, turn from our sinful ways, believe in the Good News of the Saving Gospel, and live for Jesus Christ, Who died on the cross to save us from the curse of our sins, and rose from the dead to give us the promise of eternal life in heaven.

AMERICA, WAKE UP! SOCIALISM, ANARCHY, AND MARXISM ARE NOT THE WAY TO GO IF WE EXPECT GOD TO BLESS AMERICA! GOD REMINDS US: "BLESSED IS THE NATION WHOSE GOD IS THE LORD" (Psalm 33:12).

Rev. David V. Dissen

2021

SOLI DEO GLORIA

ABOUT THE AUTHOR

Rev. David V. Dissen was born in North Dakota, the son of Rev. Victor Herman Dissen and Lydia Dissen. He is married to Judy, his wife of over 50 years.

Dissen attended public Elementary School and Junior High in North Dakota and graduated from High School in Burley, Idaho, in 1951. He attended Concordia Lutheran College in Milwaukee, Wisconsin (now Concordia University, Mequon, Wisconsin) from 1951 to 1954. He entered Concordia Seminary, St. Louis, Missouri, in the Fall semester of 1954.

His vicarage was spent in Havana, Cuba from 1957 to 1958. He graduated from Concordia Seminary in May of 1959. His first assignment was a dual pastorate at First Lutheran in Salida, Colorado, and Good Shepherd Lutheran in Leadville, Colorado. He also served at Trinity Lutheran in Beloit, Wisconsin; Zion Lutheran in South Chicago, Illinois; First Lutheran in Clearwater, Florida; and Trinity Lutheran Church in Cape Girardeau, Missouri, where he retired from full-time active ministry in 1998.

While serving congregations, Dissen worked in various capacities on behalf of the Circuit. On the District level, he served as the 1st and 2nd Vice-President of the Missouri District; Chairman of the Missouri District Board for Missions; served on the Board for Social Ministry, Crisis Counseling and other various committees; represented the Missouri District at the Intentional Interim Pastoral Ministry Conference; and was a participant in the Synodical Resolution Dispute Seminar (Conciliator Training Program).

Positions in which he has served on the Synodical Level include the Board of Regents at Concordia Seminary, St. Louis, for two six-year terms; Secretary of the Committee for Convention Nominations; Task Force on Synodical Conflict Resolution; The Adult Education Committee; Standing Committee for Congregational Administration; the President's Advisory Council of Concordia, River Forest, Illinois (now Concordia University Chicago); Voting Delegate or Advisory Delegate to Synodical Conventions on many occasions; Devotional Leader for a week-long Missionary Retreat in Venezuela; Devotional Leader at the First Annual Pieper Lectures at the

St. Louis Seminary, sponsored by the Concordia Historical Institute in St. Louis; Devotional Leader for a Synodical Convention; and Guest Presenter at different Vicarage Supervisor's Conferences. He also served as an Adjunct Professor at Concordia Seminary in his role as an advisor to 19 vicars – either from St. Louis or Concordia Theological Seminary, Fort Wayne, Indiana, helping them in their on-going pastoral formation by guiding and supervising them in their one year of on-hands, practical parish work.

Dissen served as the first president of the International Foundation for Confessional Lutheran Research (IFCLR) which began with "seed money" from a generous gift from Mr. and Mrs. (Charlotte) Martin Roth who were members at Trinity Lutheran in Cape Girardeau during his pastorate. The IFCLR, whose Executive Director was the now sainted Dr. Robert Preus, was started by the Roth's to promote orthodox and Confessional Lutheranism throughout the world. One of the first projects of the IFCLR was to embark on the publication of a 13-volume CONFESSIONAL LUTHERAN DOGMATICS series. The first two volumes published by the IFCLR were *Christology* (by David P. Scaer) in 1989 and *The Church* (by Kurt Marquart) in 1990. After that, the IFCLR "morphed" into what is now called "Luther Academy." By the grace of God, Luther Academy continues to promote orthodox Confessional Lutheranism world-wide.

Dissen has been involved in mass media radio ministry in every one of his parishes, starting a Sunday morning radio ministry at Zion Lutheran in South Chicago and First Lutheran in Clearwater, Florida. He began a Sunday TV Ministry called "Living Hope" at Trinity Lutheran in 1983. which is still being televised in 2021.

In his retirement, Dissen provided leadership in launching Saxony Lutheran High School in Southeast Missouri, which has grown from seven to around 220 students. He served about a dozen congregations as vacancy pastor and served for 11 years as the Vacancy Pastor of Lutheran Chapel of Hope, which is the Campus Ministry of the LCMS at Southeast Missouri State University in Cape Girardeau, Missouri. In his local community, Dissen served the city of Cape Girardeau as a Chaplain on the Cape Fire and Police Departments for several decades.

Made in the USA
Coppell, TX
31 July 2022

80712135R00090